1982

FIGHTING RED CLOUD'S WARRIORS

CHIEF "RED CLOUD", WHOSE CONSTANT SIEGE OF FORT PHIL
KEARNEY COMPELLED THE GOVERNMENT TO ABANDON THE
COUNTRY. PHOTO COURTESY CAPT. J. H. COOK, AGATE, NEB.

"THE FRONTIER SERIES"

Fighting Red Cloud's Warriors

True Tales of Indian Days When the
West Was Young

By E. A. BRININSTOOL

(Honorary Companion "Order of Indian Wars,"
Author: "Trail Dust of a Maverick,"
"A Trooper With Custer;" Co-
author "The Bozeman Trail"

COOPER SQUARE PUBLISHERS, INC.
New York
1975

Originally Published 1926
Published 1975 by Cooper Square Publishers, Inc.
59 Fourth Avenue, New York, N. Y. 10003

Printed in the United States of America
by Sentry Press, Inc., New York, N. Y. 10013

Library of Congress Cataloging in Publication Data

Brininstool, Earl Alonzo, 1870-1957.
    Fighting Red Cloud's warriors.
    Reprint of the 1926 ed. published by Hunter-Trader-
Trapper Co., Columbus, Ohio, which was issued as v. 2
of the Frontier series.
    1. Indians of North America—Wars—1866-1895.
2. Red Cloud, Sioux chief, 1822-1909. 3. Frontier
and pioneer life—The West. I. Title. II. Series:
The Frontier series (Columbus, O., 1925-   ). v. 2.
E83.866.B85   1975   917.8'03'2   74-12557
ISBN 0-8154-0499-9

DEDICATION

To my dear friend, Mrs. Mary E. Graham, now (1926) in her 87th year; the first white woman to settle in northwestern Nebraska; champion of the American Indian; personal friend of that great Sioux chieftain and warrior, RED CLOUD; pioneer woman of distinction; who has encouraged and aided me in the writing of these Western historical sketches, this volume is most affectionately dedicated.

PREFACE

THE winning of the West was no child's play! It was war — war of the most brutal and inhuman type on the part of both Indians and whites. The Indian was fighting for his home, his commissary, his lands—lands ceded him through solemn treaty with the United States government — and what man, of any nation (if he is any sort of man) will not fight "for home and native land"?

The white man fought to advance the cause of civilization, irrespective (in most instances) of the rights of the Indian, and without regard to his future existence. Civilization won — and to civilization's shame, it was at the cost of unnumbered thousands of lives and the shedding of much human blood of both whites and reds.

I am not a believer in the old adage that "the only good Indian is a dead Indian." My sympathy is with the red man. The early white traders who trafficked with the Indian were, as a rule, a class of men of little conscience and few scruples, who would stoop to any deceit or trickery to rob the Indian of his furs and pelts. It was the early trader who introduced whiskey among the Indian tribes; who, through fraud and knavery, turned the red man against the whites of whatever class. This was the beginning of the hatred and contempt which made all white men, good or bad, soon look alike to the warring savage.

(9)

Unscrupulous Indian agents, tricky post traders, unprincipled government officials at Washington, and a few — a very few — inhuman army officers fed fuel to the flame of contempt which quickly spread through the Indian tribes of the far West. Briefly, the whole situation can be summed up in these five words: *"The white man wanted it!"*

In this volume of the *"Frontier Series"* I have written of a few of the most noted battles between the red man and the white man. As in the previous volume, no fiction is employed in these pages. Every incident related actually occurred, and is a part of the history of the old West. Some biographical sketches of noted frontier characters are included. The chapter on the destruction of the buffalo may well make the present-day sportsman pause and reflect.

Acknowledgments are due the following friends for facts and information furnished me in the preparation of some portions of this volume: Capt. Jas. H. Cook, Sergt. Samuel Gibson, Sigmund Shlesinger, Mrs. Olive K. Dixon, Jeff C. Riddle, Jesse Brown, Francis W. Hilton.

Volume 3 of the *"Frontier Series"* already is in course of preparation. It will contain accounts of other noted Indian battles, and a comprehensive sketch of that remarkable frontiersman, "California Joe."

Other volumes doubtless will be added to the series as historical data in a more correct form than has yet appeared in print, is brought to light through correspondence and research. And there is plenty of room for correction in what has heretofore been written about Indian warfare—correction long due the Indian, which it is my intention to present in its true light as many untruths are uncovered.

E. A. BRININSTOOL.

Los Angeles, Cal., 1926.

CONTENTS

ILLUSTRATIONS

(15)

CHAPTER I

THE TRAGEDY OF FORT PHIL KEARNEY

HOW THE RASHNESS OF CAPT. WM. J. FETTERMAN
RESULTED IN THE ANNIHILATION OF HIS ENTIRE
COMMAND OF EIGHTY-ONE MEN.

O N the highway between Sheridan and Buffalo, in the present state of Wyoming, and about twenty-three miles southeast of the former city, stands an unpretentious monument about fifteen feet high, built of the rough cobblestones picked up in the immediate vicinity. Across the face of this rugged shaft is fastened a bronze shield bearing the following inscription:

ON THIS FIELD ON THE 21ST DAY OF
DECEMBER, 1866,

THREE COMMISSIONED OFFICERS AND SEVENTY-SIX PRIVATES OF THE 18TH U. S. INFANTRY AND OF THE 2D U. S. CAVALRY, UNDER THE COMMAND OF CAPT. BREVET-LT. COL. WM. J. FETTERMAN, WERE KILLED BY AN OVERWHELMING FORCE OF SIOUX UNDER COMMAND OF RED CLOUD.

THERE WERE NO SURVIVORS.

In order to fully understand the details of this great frontier tragedy — second only to the Custer fight in horror — let us hark back a bit and investigate the reason therefor. Let us see who was to blame — the Indians or the United States government.

Montana, in the early '60's, was fast recognized as a great gold-bearing section, and emigrants, miners, adventurers and home-seekers were attempting to get into that far-away territory by the quickest and safest route. The Indians were bad — hordes of people were traveling through the best of their hunting grounds, killing off their game and taking away their own sustenance. Almost every wagon train was attacked. Traveling in small parties was out of the question.

By 1866 the government had arrived at the conclusion that something must be done toward treating with the Indians in order that these Western-bound "pilgrims" might have safe traveling into Montana. and the northwest. The Sioux held undisputed sway over the region east of the Big Horn mountains and south to the Platte River.

Red Cloud, the great war-chief of the Sioux, objected to making any such treaty as was proposed by the government. He did not want any wagon road built through his hunting grounds, nor any forts erected or soldiers maintained to safeguard such a road. He claimed that it was the last and best hunting grounds of the Sioux tribe, and that under no circumstances would he accede to the demands of the authorities at Washington, that a wagon road be opened into the Montana country.

THE COBBLESTONE MONUMENT ON "MASSACRE HILL" TO VICTIMS
OF THE FETTERMAN DISASTER.   PHOTO BY E. A. BRININSTOOL.

However, Red Cloud consented to attend a council which was held about the middle of June, 1866, at Fort Laramie. This was presided over by Col. Henry B. Carrington of the 18th U. S. Infantry. In the midst of the negotiations — many of the Indians were in favor of the road — Red Cloud sprang into the center of the council ring, pointed a finger at Col. Carrington and exclaimed in ringing tones:

"You are the White Eagle who has come to steal the road! The Great Father sends us presents and wants us to sell him the road, *but the white chief comes with soldiers to steal it before the Indian says yes or no!* I will talk with you no more! I will go, now, and I will fight you! As long as I live I will fight for the last hunting grounds of my people!" And turning on his heel, with head erect and eye flashing fire, Red Cloud stalked majestically out of the council, followed by many of his leading sub-chiefs, and immediately prepared to go on the war-path.

This was an open threat, but the government treated it lightly, and immediately prepared to invade Red Cloud's forbidden territory. The great chief had given warning that he would not object to having Fort Connor (later named Fort Reno) stand along the Bozeman Trail, away to the northwest, but that any attempt to build forts or maintain soldiers north of that point would be followed by immediate war, and that he "would kill every white man who went north of Crazy Woman's Fork."

Col. Carrington's instructions from the government were to restock and better equip the post, later known as Fort Reno, then start north and build two more forts between that point and the Montana line, at places which he should select himself. He started from Fort Kearney, Nebraska, May 19, 1866, with a great retinue, fully equipped with every necessary article for carrying out the government's wishes, and July 14th arrived at the junction of Big and Little Piney creeks, in the present state of Wyoming. Here he began the erection of the first post, which was called Fort Phil Kearney, in honor of a noted Federal army officer killed in the Civil War. In August another fort.was erected ninety-one miles north of Fort Phil Kearney, called Fort C. F. Smith. This story, however, deals only with the former post.

Red Cloud, meantime, was not idle. He gathered together a great army of his best fighting warriors, and prepared to make it exceedingly interesting for Col. Carrington. While the fort was in process of construction he lost no opportunity to harass and bother the troops in every possible manner. He had from 2,500 to 4,000 warriors in the field, commanded in person by himself, American Horse, Big Mouth, Young-Man-Afraid-of-His-Horses and other noted chiefs of the Sioux tribe.

The fort was built in the shape of a rectangle, 600 x 800 feet, inclosed with a formidable stockade made of heavy pine logs, placed four feet in the ground, and standing eight feet high in the clear.

In order to secure the necessary logs and lumber for the erection of the many buildings, it was necessary to send wood trains six or seven miles from the post back to the mountains where timber was

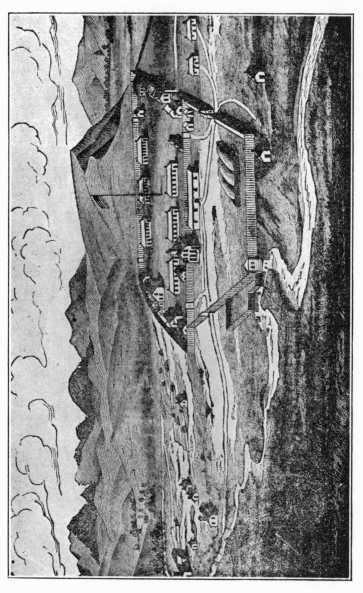

FORT PHIL KEARNEY FROM AN OLD DRAWING. ERECTED 1866, ABANDONED BY THE GOVERNMENT 1868.

available. All these trains were heavily guarded, yet in spite of the utmost caution, many soldiers were cut off and killed by little war parties.

To summarize the matter: During the first six months of fighting, from the first of August to the close of the year 1866, Red Cloud's warriors killed 154 persons, including soldiers and citizens, wounded twenty more and captured nearly 700 animals — cattle, mules, horses — while fifty-one demonstrations were made by the Indians in force in front of the fort, and every wagon train that went over the Bozeman Road was attacked. So much for Red Cloud's activity.

Early in December the fort was in the last stages of completion. On the 6th, the wood train was again attacked. A party was sent to its relief from the fort, and in the skirmish which ensued Lieut. Bingham and Sergeant Bowers were killed and five soldiers wounded.

And on December 8th, President Andrew Johnson congratulated Congress that treaties had been effected with the warring Indians and that *"all was at peace"* in the Northwest! Little did the Washington solons realize the storm which was gathering and which was to burst about their heads with telling force!

By December 19th, it was estimated by Col. Carrington that one more large wood train could bring in all the necessary logs for the completion of the hospital building, which was the last bit of work necessary before the fort could be called actually finished.

The prudent policy of Col. Carrington in fighting

the Indians was scoffed at by many of his younger
officers, particularly Capt. Wm. J. Fetterman and
Capt. Frederick Brown, who were constantly im-
portuning the Commanding Officer that they be allowed to start out with eighty or a hundred men
and drive the Indians out of the country. "Give me
eighty men," exclaimed Fetterman, "and I will ride
through the Sioux nation."

Carrington, however, had foresight enough to see
the folly of such foolish talk. He sternly forbade
any such scheme, warning his officers that they were
fighting men just as cunning in military strategy
as themselves, and who were far better posted on
the lay of the land, and besides, his entire command was at times outnumbered fifty to one. Fetterman and Brown secretly smiled at the caution
of their commander.

It is a matter of conjecture to this day why Red
Cloud never made a direct attack upon the post with
his whole available force. Had he done so and maintained the siege, it is not unlikely that he would
have been successful. Carrington's whole available
fighting force numbered only about three hundred
and fifty men at its most populous period. His ammunition was likewise running low, at one time
there being but forty rounds per man available. No
help or relief could be expected in the event of an
attack upon the post, as the nearest point where
soldiers were available was at Fort Laramie, 236
miles to the southeast. There was, of course, no
telegraphic communication with the outside world,
and any appeal for reinforcements would have to
be made by courier, through a country swarming
with hostile Indians.

GRAVES OF THE 81 VICTIMS OF THE FETTERMAN DISASTER.
PHOTO BY E. A. BRININSTOOL.

SITE OF FORT PHIL KEARNEY.   THE OLD STOCKADED POST STOOD
ON THE PLATEAU BEHIND THE TWO TREES.   PHOTO BY E. A.
BRININSTOOL.

On December 21st, about 11 o'clock in the morning, the lookout on Pilot Hill, near the fort (where a watch was constantly maintained) signaled that the wood train which was enroute to the fort from the pinery, was again corraled and being attacked, about a mile and a half from the fort.

Captain Fetterman was at that moment walking up and down in front of his quarters. Col. Carrington immediately organized a detachment to go to the relief of the wood train. Fetterman, claiming his seniority, asked and was given command of this party, which was composed — including himself — of eighty-one men — just the number with which Fetterman had boasted he "could ride through the Sioux nation."

Among the relief party were two civilians named Wheatley and Fisher, frontiersmen, living at the fort. These men had lately come into possession of Henry repeating rifles — an arm just on the market, and possessed of wonderful rapidity of fire. It was a magazine gun holding sixteen metallic cartridges. They were very anxious to try the new arm against the Indians and were looked upon as a formidable addition to Fetterman's party.

When the command was ready to start, Col. Carrington gave Fetterman strict and positive instructions as to what his movements were to be. He was ordered to relieve the wood train, but on no account whatever to pursue the Indians beyond a certain point known as Lodge Trail Ridge. Well knowing Fetterman's enthusiasm and recklessness when after Indians, and still fearful that his orders might not be thoroughly understood and obeyed, Col. Carrington sprang upon the sentry platform inside the stockade, and shouted after Fetterman: *"Remember, on no account whatever must you pursue the Indians beyond Lodge Trail Ridge."* Fetterman made no reply.

After leaving the fort, Fetterman did not go directly to the wood train, but led his men to a point known as Peno Valley, possibly thinking he could get in the rear of the Indians and wipe them out between his own troops and the wood train guard. His move was noted at the fort by Col. Carrington, who was watching everything through his field glasses, but as it did not involve any disobedience of orders, caused no apprehension — indeed, it was agreed that it might be a good tactical maneuver.

The minute the savages noted Fetterman's command leaving the fort, they withdrew and ceased their attack on the wood train, which at once broke corral and started on toward the fort, where it arrived without further molestation. By this time Fetterman's command was out of sight of the watchers at the post, and serious apprehension began to be immediately felt.

No surgeon had been sent with his command, so a few minutes after Fetterman's departure Surgeon Hines was instructed by Carrington to hasten and join the relief party. He left, but soon returned with the startling information that when he tried to cross Peno Valley he found it swarming with Indians, who were concentrating there and upon Lodge Trail Ridge, and that he could see nothing whatever of Fetterman's command.

MARKER ON SITE OF FORT PHIL KEARNEY. PHOTO COURTESY
DR. GRACE RAYMOND HEBARD, LARAMIE, WYO.

(28)

The fears of the watchers at the fort were realized when, about noon, heavy firing was heard in the direction of Lodge Trail Ridge, which was about five miles away. This soon broke into the roar of battle, and it was plainly evident that Fetterman had run into a hornet's nest.

Col. Carrington immediately made up another detachment commanded by Capt. Tenodore Ten Eyck, an officer of known caution, military skill and bravery, consisting of fifty-four of the infantry. He took a couple of wagons along with his party. The command left the fort on the run.

The whole garrison was now on the alert. Extra ammunition was immediately opened, all prisoners were released from the guardhouse and every available man armed and placed on duty.

Ten Eyck's men hurried toward Lodge Trail Ridge. When they arrived, they could see nothing of the Fetterman party. He at once sent an orderly back to the fort with the information that the entire valley on the other side of the ridge was full of yelling, exultant savages who were challenging him to come down and fight. All firing had stopped. Ten Eyck requested that a howitzer be sent him to clear the valley of Indians.

Carrington sent back word by the courier that forty more men, with three thousand extra rounds of ammunition, were on the way to join him; that he must unite with Fetterman, keep his men well in hand, fire slowly, and both commands return to the fort at once. No howitzer could be sent, as no horses could be spared to haul it.

After the forty extra men had joined Ten Eyck,

he marched cautiously up Lodge Trail Ridge, the Indians giving way before him. He estimated the fighting strength of the savages at fully 2,000, and was too prudent an officer to accept the challenge to come down into the valley while they were there. He stood on the defensive on the hill until the Indians had left. Then, after satisfying himself that a forward movement was safe, he marched over the ridge and down into Peno Valley, and to the bare lower ridge over which ran the Bozeman Road.

There a most shocking sight presented itself. Within a little rocky enclosure were found forty-nine bodies of the Fetterman command, stripped, shot full of arrows, scalped, hacked and mutilated in a most fiendish manner. There were no evidences of a great struggle right there, and close investigation disclosed the fact that all but four of the men had been killed with clubs, tomahawks, stones, or spears. Four bodies alone showed bullet marks, and these may have been self-inflicted.

Brown and Fetterman were found lying side by side with bullet holes through their heads. It was known that both had sworn to commit suicide rather than to ever fall into Indian hands, although it has been given out by many historians that doubtless they had stood side by side and shot each other.*

---

* Years later, Chief American Horse, then passing his last days at Pine Ridge reservation, South Dakota, confided to Capt. James H. Cook, his close white friend, and also an intimate friend of mine, that he was a prominent leader in the Fetterman fight, which was commanded by Red Cloud. American Horse stated that he personally killed Capt. Fetterman, riding up behind him and knocking him from his horse with a war-club and finishing him with his knife. This chief, as

Ten Eyck had brought wagons along, and without stopping to make further investigation, the bodies of the forty-nine dead men were loaded into the wagons and the return to the fort made in safety. The fate of the other thirty-two men of the command he did not know, but it was safe to suppose that all had been killed.

The inmates of the fort were horror-stricken at this appalling calamity. Nearly one-fourth of the entire command at the post had been wiped out. Guards were doubled. A night attack was looked upon as a surety. No man slept, and the women and little children at the fort, of which there were several, were filled with terror. The night passed, however, without an alarm.

The next morning Carrington called a council of officers as to the wisdom of sending out another party to search for the missing thirty-two of Fetterman's command. Most of them were against such a move. There were no more men to be sacrificed. But Col. Carrington was firm in his declaration that he would in person make such an attempt if it cost him his own life. He had no trouble to get followers   Every soldier wanted to join his party.

well as others of the Sioux, stated that the Fetterman command seemed completely terror-stricken when they saw how vastly they were outnumbered; that they made no attempt to fight back, save in the cases of some of the more experienced soldiers, and that the Indians killed them with clubs, stones, hatchets, etc., like sheep. This story may or may not be true, but I am inclined to believe it because of the close intimacy between Capt. Cook and all the leading Sioux chiefs at Pine Ridge during their latter days, when they were more inclined to talk freely of their days of battle.

GEN. H. B. CARRINGTON. HE PLANNED AND BUILT FORT PHIL
KEARNEY IN JULY, 1866. DIED, 1912.

Col. Carrington left positive orders that in case of an attack upon the post while he was absent, the women and children were to be placed in the ammunition magazine, with an officer pledged not to allow them to be captured alive, and in case of a successful assault by the Indians, this officer was to apply the match and blow all to eternity.

Passing the spot where the first forty-nine bodies were found, Carrington presently came upon evidences of a great struggle and fierce hand-to-hand fighting. Bodies were strung along the road clear to the western end farthest from the fort. Behind a little pile of rocks were found the bodies of Wheatley and Fisher, the two frontiersmen who accompanied Fetterman, armed with the Henry repeating rifles. By the side of one, fifty empty shells were counted, and nearly that number by the other. Wheatley's body fairly bristled with 105 arrows! In front of these two men were counted sixty great blood clots on the snow, and a great number of dead ponies, showing the deadly accuracy of their modern weapons. The remains of every one of the missing thirty-two were accounted for — all stripped naked, scalped and mutilated beyond recognition in a ghastly and revolting manner.

Fetterman had disobeyed his orders. Instead of returning to the fort after the wood train had been relieved, he had gone in pursuit of the Indians, who had cunningly led him into an ambush, then fell upon him like an avalanche and annihilated his entire command within twenty minutes. What folly in believing that "with eighty or a hundred men he could ride through the Sioux nation!"

"PORTUGEE" PHILLIPS, THE COURIER WHO SAVED FORT PHIL
KEARNEY FROM DISASTER. DIED IN CHEYENNE, WYOMING, IN
THE EARLY '80s.

The Indian loss in the fight was quite severe but never definitely known.*

Carrington collected all of the dead and returned to the fort without even catching sight of an Indian.

That night a frightful blizzard broke loose, the thermometer dropped to more than 25 degrees below zero and the snow piled so rapidly against the stockade that forces of men worked in fifteen-minute shifts shoveling it away lest the drifts attain such a height that the Indians could climb over the stockade. But the severity of the weather kept the Indians within their own shelters. Guards and snow shovelers were changed every fifteen minutes, and even at that, many of them were badly frostbitten. Lights burned in all the quarters, and everybody fully expected an attack to be made upon the post after this great bloody victory by Red Cloud's warriors.

It was imperative that help be summoned at once from Fort Laramie, and the news of the frightful massacre given to the Washington authorities. This could only be done by courier. Carrington called for a man with the required nerve. Nobody would volunteer from among the troops. Finally a frontiersman known as "Portugee" Phillips, well-trained to Indian fighting and with accurate knowledge of the country, stepped forward and said that as long as no one else would volunteer, he would go himself. It meant a ride of 236 miles through a country swarming with hostile Indians, where constant

---

*American Horse told Capt. Cook that only about eleven of their warriors were killed, but that great numbers were wounded.

Captain Fetterman, who led the troops in the disastrous fight of December 21, 1866

Captain Ten Eyck, who was sent to the relief of Captain Fetterman

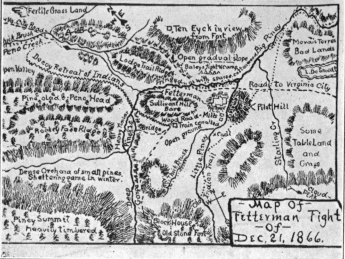

watchfulness was necessary, with snowdrifts that had completely obliterated the trails, and in zero weather. All Phillips asked for was the swiftest horse at the post. This was a blooded animal owned by Col. Carrington himself.

This request was instantly granted by the colonel, and at midnight, with only a few crackers for himself and a hatful of feed for his horse, Phillips rode out through a little side gate of the stockade and slipped away into the howling storm. Everyone at the post expected that he would be apprehended before he had gone a hundred yards, but there was no demonstration. Apparently the Indians were flushed with their first bloody victory and felt that they could take their time to finish the balance of the command at the "hated fort on the Little Piney," as it was known among the savages.

I have always looked upon this ride of John ("Portugee") Phillips as the greatest and most daring in all the annals of American history. The ride of Paul Revere, to give notice of the approach of the British, was a summer's day canter in comparison. To leave out all the thrilling details — the cold, hunger, fatigue, which Phillips and his faithful horse endured, as well as the constant watchfulness necessary to avoid capture, he arrived at Fort Laramie on Christmas eve, December 24th, while a great ball was in progress at "Bedlam," the building where all the post activities and social functions were held. The daring rider reeled from his saddle on the parade ground, as his gallant horse dropped dead under him, and staggered into the midst of the festivities — a gigantic, swaying figure, swathed from head to foot in buffalo overcoat, leggins and cap. Gasping incoherently the news of the catastrophe at Fort Phil Kearney, he dropped in a dead faint from over-exposure and exhaustion.

There was a wire east from Fort Laramie, and the news of the appalling disaster was immediately spread broadcast. It caused a gasp of horror to sweep over the country. In spite of the fact that Col. Carrington had conducted himself in every way as a brave, prudent, cautious, skillful, capable soldier, it was, of course, necessary that someone be made "the goat." He was immediately relieved of the command of Fort Phil Kearney by Gen. Philip St. George Cooke, Department Commander at Omaha — to whom, by the way, Carrington had constantly importuned for improved arms, more men and more ammunition, all requests being promptly turned down.

Col. Carrington was notified that he must report at Fort Casper, several days' journey to the south, at a certain date. He was obliged to leave Fort Phil Kearney early in January, 1867, when the thermometer stood at forty degrees below zero, with his wife, two small children and a guard. So frightful was the weather that some of the teamsters were so badly frozen by the time Fort Reno was reached, that amputation of the lower limbs of one or two was necessary; one of the teamsters died, and several days elapsed before Carrington's party was able to proceed on to Fort Casper.

Col. Carrington at once demanded a full and complete investigation of his conduct as commander of Fort Phil Kearney. It was *twenty years* before the

Washington authorities listened to his appeal and granted him a hearing, at which he was completely exonerated from all charges of incompetency, and it was proved beyond question that he at all times had acted wisely, cautiously, prudently and ably in all his engagements with the Indians, and that the entire blame for the Fetterman disaster was through that officer's flat disobedience of orders and his own rashness and desire to "show" Carrington his ability as an Indian fighter, thus sacrificing his entire command.

Two years later the government arrived at the conclusion that Chief Red Cloud was too strategic and able a warrior to fight against.   Another conference was called, at which Red Cloud reiterated his demands that the entire country be abandoned by the government, all the troops withdrawn and the forts dismantled.   He would listen to no other sort of a compromise.   The government, wisely concluding that "discretion was the better part of valor," came to Red Cloud's terms.   In August, 1868, Fort Phil Kearney was abandoned.   Before the troops had marched a mile from the post, the Indians swarmed out of the ravines and applied the torch, and from the distant hills the soldiers watched the great structure go up in smoke.

The site of this noted frontier fort is on land now owned by George Geier, the land being originally homesteaded in 1878 by the late Judge Thomas J. Foster of Sheridan, Wyoming.   In 1913 the author made a visit to the spot accompanied by Judge Foster.   Where had been the parade ground of the old post was found a fine alfalfa field.   Scattered

INSCRIPTION ON IRON TABLET ON FETTERMAN MASSACRE MONU-
MENT. PHOTO BY E. A. BRININSTOOL.

about were yet the remnants of some of the old stoves and baking ovens used by the troops, and the east line of the old stockade was yet discernible. A three-foot section of one of the original logs was sticking out of the ground, and permission was given to cut this off and bring it home, and today this blackened, well-worn bit of tough pine stands in a case in the author's den, a grim reminder of one of the greatest tragedies on the Western frontier.

In 1908, Col. Carrington, then in his 86th year, made a trip from his distant Massachusetts home, to the site of Fort Phil Kearney for the purpose of dedicating the cobblestone monument on "Massacre Hill." Chief Red Cloud, then aged, blind and infirm, at Pine Ridge reservation, was also most earnestly requested to attend the ceremonies, but owing to his advanced age and poor health, said that while he would have been glad to be present and shake the hand of the great White Chief, his former foe, his health would not permit. Col. Carrington died in 1912, and Chief Red Cloud in 1910. The state of Wyoming has placed a suitable marker on the site of the old fort, and today automobiles spin along the highway where, in 1866, Red Cloud's warriors laid in wait for scalps.

CHAPTER II

THE "WAGON-BOX FIGHT"

THIRTY-TWO AGAINST THREE THOUSAND — AN UNPAR-
ALLELED INDIAN BATTLE

A S one sits at his ease in a palatial Pullman car
nowadays and is whisked across the conti-
nent, through what, fifty to sixty years ago,
was known as the "Plains country," he little realizes
the tremendous sacrifice of life, the unparalleled
suffering, the terrible privation, exposure and hardships endured by the "men who made the West."

The author refers now, more especially, to the
men of the Regular Army, who, for the mere pittance of $13 a month, marched, fought and bivou-
acked over the "Great American Desert," established forts in the face of almost certain death,
fought the hordes of savage warriors in their own
country, protected the slowly-crawling prairie
schooners and emigrant trains, and kept the line of
travel open for the overland stages. It was the
"Regular Army man" who bore the brunt of the advance of civilization. All honor to these men! Let
the memory of their brave deeds and gallant sac-
rifices be never forgotten, but kept constantly before
the minds of the rising generation of school children, who know — alas! — too little of the "winning of the West."

The year 1866 was known as "the bloody year on the Plains." The savages were almost constantly on the warpath; stage travel was, for a time, completely at a standstill. The Indians were seeking to prevent the encroachment of the whites into their favorite hunting grounds, or the establishing of ranches in the fertile valleys of the many beautiful streams in the present state of Wyoming.

Travel into the gold fields of Montana was especially heavy, particularly so by way of the Bozeman Trail, which had just been opened. And the Bozeman Trail led through what was then the last and best hunting grounds of the Sioux. The white-topped wagons were, in the eyes of the Sioux, on a par with a red rag to a bull. The encroachment of the whites meant that the game would be frightened and driven out of the country, and this meant the annihilation of the commissary of the Indians — and what man, red or white, will not fight for his subsistence!

Chief Red Cloud — that greatest of fighting men of red blood — keen, brainy, crafty, a born general in war, realized far better than did any of his sub-chiefs, what this white invasion of the West would mean in a short time to the Indian, and it was to protect what he considered the last and choicest hunting grounds of his tribe, that he began a war of extermination against the whites.

In those days old Fort Laramie was the "jumping-off place." After that point was passed, skillful frontiersmanship was absolutely essential to prevent a surprise, an attack and complete annihilation by the red men. The government was appealed to

FREDERIC CLAUS, ONE OF THE DEFENDERS OF THE WAGON BOX CORRAL, NOW LIVING IN LINCOLN, NEBR.

for soldiers to protect the trails and to insure safe passage for the hundreds of wagon-trains bound for the Montana country and the northwest.

Briefly, it was finally decided to send an expedition, thoroughly equipped, to establish military posts along the route of travel to the northwest of Fort Laramie, over the Bozeman Trail. To this end, Col. Henry B. Carrington, of the 18th U. S. Infantry, was instructed to proceed from Fort Kearney, Nebraska, with all the necessary troops and equipment, for that purpose.

It is not the intention, in this small space, to recount the experiences of the Carrington Expedition on its way to what was then a veritable "terra incognito,"— a land as unknown as was the heart of Africa. This unknown and unsettled country comprised the present state of Wyoming. Carrington's instructions were to proceed to old Fort Connor, and there to restock and rebuild that post, garrison it and make it the southern post of the Bozeman Trail. He was then to proceed northward and build and garrison two more forts, about 100 miles apart. It was thus believed that protection could be guaranteed to the newcomers into the Montana country.

Carrington's expedition left Fort Kearney, Nebraska, May 19, 1866, with the noted Jim Bridger as chief guide. Fort Laramie was reached on the 16th of June. Here were assembled thousands of Sioux Indians, headed by Chief Red Cloud, to hold a peace council with some Commissioners from Washington. This was for the purpose of endeavoring to secure passage through the Sioux country, without molestation, and to gain the consent of the

Indians to erect and maintain the proposed military posts.

But Chief Red Cloud and his "right bower," Young-Man-Afraid-of-His-Horses, refused to consider the proposition. Red Cloud charged the government with "stealing the country before the red man had a chance to say yes or no." Both chiefs stalked out of the council, shouting defiance, refusing any of the presents which has been offered them, and swearing they would "kill every white man who passed beyond Crazy Woman's Fork of the Powder River." They said they would not object to the garrisoning of old Fort Connor, but that under no circumstances would they consent that Carrington build any more forts north of that point. It would mean war to the knife if he did.

But Carrington paid no attention to these threats. He was there under orders from Washington to go ahead — and go ahead he did. Fort Connor was garrisoned and provisioned, and the name changed to Fort Reno, after which Carrington started north to locate sites for the two other proposed military posts.

On July 14th, the expedition reached a point nearly one hundred miles north of Fort Reno which appealed to Col. Carrington as best located for the building of the first fort. It was at the forks of Big and Little Piney Creeks. This spot today is a part of the ranch of George Geier, and is situated twenty-three miles southeast of the city of Sheridan, Wyoming. The following morning, July 15th, logging parties were detailed, and the erection of Fort Phil Kearney was begun.

CAPT. JAMES W. POWELL, IN COMMAND OF THE DEFENDERS OF
THE WAGON BOX CORRAL.

Among the soldiers who left Fort Kearney, Nebraska, with the expedition, was Sergt. Samuel Gibson, today a resident of Bellevue, Nebraska. The author has talked by the hour with Sergeant Gibson of his experiences through those trying days, and the sergeant here recounts them in his own way:

"I was born in England in 1849, and resided there until 1865, when my father and his family removed to the United States. In April, 1866, I enlisted in the United States army at Cleveland, Ohio. I was assigned to Company C, second battalion, 18th U. S. Infantry, at Fort Kearney, Nebraska, in May, where I became a member of the Carrington Expedition. We marched across the Plains to Julesburg, Colorado, where we crossed the South Platte river hand over hand on a thick rope stretched across the river — nine hundred of us.

"From Julesburg we marched through Ash Hollow and across the Platte Valley to Fort Laramie, where we rested three or four days. At this point some Indian Commissioners were holding a council with Red Cloud and Young-Man-Afraid-of-His-Horses, Sioux chiefs, to obtain their consent to build some forts through the Indian's favorite hunting grounds along the Bozeman Trail, close to the Big Horn mountains. Col. Carrington was sent for to be present at this council with the Commissioners.

"When Red Cloud was told that Carrington was the man who was going in command of the soldiers to build those forts, he grabbed his rifle and shook it in the faces of the Commissioners, declaring that the soldiers should not pass through his favorite hunting grounds, and that he would kill every soldier of the command, and wage a war of extermination against all white invaders.

"The Commissioners took no notice of Red Cloud's threats, and Col. Carrington proceeded to carry out his orders.

"The expedition reached old Fort Connor (later called Fort Reno) on June 28th. Here we relieved two companies of the Fifth U. S. Infantry (galvanized Yankees*) and two troops of the 11th Ohio Cavalry. We left this post on July 9th, and arrived at the forks of the Piney Creeks on July 14th. On July 15th, Col. Carrington located the plateau on which we built historic Fort Phil Kearney — and from that time on our troubles commenced. The fort was located seven miles from the Big Horn mountains.

"Not a hostile Indian had we seen until after we arrived at the Piney Creeks; but as soon as we began to send out logging trains to bring in the necessary timber for the erection of a stockade and the barracks and other buildings, there was continual fighting. The Indians attacked our logging parties nine times between July 14th and July 29th, and when we went into the pineries, seven miles distant, we never knew from one day to the next if we would come back dead or alive.

"In August, two of our men, Gilchrist and Johnson, were lariated by the Indians while returning

---

* "Galvanized Yankees" was a term applied to captured Confederate soldiers who were sent west to fight Indians in preference to military imprisonment in the East.

SERGT. SAMUEL S. GIBSON.   PHOTO BY E. A. BRININSTOOL.

(50)

to the post from the hay camp. They were pulled from their horses and tortured to death over a slow fire. This occurred about eight to ten miles down Big Piney Creek. We found their skulls and portions of their skeletons a week later, as well as one of their broken rifles.

"This is how the red devils harassed us every day while we were building the fort. They ran off our beef herd early in September, also twenty-five or thirty mules, and attacked every wagon-train that came up the Bozeman Trail, sometimes keeping these trains corraled three and four days between watering places, so that men and animals suffered extremely from thirst. Every wagon train on its way to Virginia City or Last Chance Gulch lost from two to half a dozen men, besides a great many draught animals.

"Yet in spite of all this, we had to keep going to the pineries every day for logs. Each morning our wood train would go seven miles west of the post to the headwaters of Big Piney Creek, (except Sundays). On that day we always had inspection of arms and clothing, in full-dress uniform.

"On October 31, 1866, our log stockade was finished. It covered a space of ground six hundred by eight hundred feet. A beautiful flag staff had been made by Drum Major Barnes of the band, assisted by Private William Daley. On that day, Col. Carrington gave us a holiday, and we witnessed the hoisting of the first garrison flag at Fort Phil Kearney.

"On December 6th, Lieut. Bingham and Sergt. Bowers were killed on the bluffs near Lodge Trail

Ridge, in an engagement with the Indians, and Lieut. Grummond barely escaped with his life, the fleetness of his horse alone preventing his massacre.

"On December 21st occurred the terrible Fetterman disaster. Captain Fetterman had been ordered, with eighty men, to relieve a wood train which had been attacked by the Sioux and forced to go into corral. The savages had the train surrounded about half way between the pinery and the fort, and the men were fighting hard. When the Fetterman detail was observed by the Indians, the attacking was abandoned and the wood train moved on toward the pinery.

"But Fetterman disobeyed Col. Carrington's orders. He did not follow the trail of the wood train. Carrington had directed him to *follow the wood train and stay with it until its return to the fort*. Fetterman led his command over Lodge Trail Ridge, right on the Bozeman Road, out of sight of the fort, where he was surrounded by about two thousand Indians, and within a very few minutes his entire command had been slaughtered to a man. All were scalped and their bodies fiendishly and most horribly mutilated.

"Captain Tenodore Ten Eyck, an officer of caution, and experienced in Indian warfare, who had been sent out by Col. Carrington after firing had been heard in the direction taken by Fetterman's command, brought in forty-five of the bodies. The next day I was in the detachment that went out under the personal command of Col. Carrington, with mule teams, and brought in the other thirty-

MAX LITTMANN, ONE OF THE DEFENDERS OF THE WAGON BOX
CORRAL. NOW A WEALTHY MANUFACTURER OF ST. LOUIS.

six bodies. Not one of them had on a stitch of clothing, except my chum, Kelly, who had enlisted with me at Cleveland, in April. Some of the bodies had as many as sixty or seventy arrows shot into them. As winter had set in all were frozen stiff. We dressed them in full uniform and buried them on Christmas day, with the weather so cold that the burial detail had to change shifts every fifteen minutes.

"Col. Carrington was blamed by the government and a criticising public for this disaster, whereas Fetterman was entirely to blame for it. I happened to be on guard at the west gate of the fort on the morning of December 21, 1866, when Fetterman and his men passed out the gate, and I distinctly heard Col. Carrington order Fetterman to follow the wood train and not leave it under any circumstances whatever.

"That is how we lived and fought for twenty-six months, with nothing to eat but hardtack and sowbelly three times a day. We had no vegetables of any sort, and we lost over thirty men who died with scurvy during that terrible winter of 1866-'67. When the Piney Creeks froze up for the winter, we did not have a chance to take a bath until they thawed out the following spring, consequently most of the enlisted men were lousy most of the time we were at Fort Phil Kearney.

"On January 1, 1867, the second battalion of the 18th U. S. Infantry was designated as a regiment, and was called the 27th U. S. Infantry. Our new colonel, John E. Smith, came up from Fort Laramie

with General Wessels — the latter having succeeded
Col. Carrington as commandant of Fort Phil Kearney.

"Colonel and Mrs. Carrington and their two small
children, and Mrs. Geo. W. Grummond, the widow
of Lieut. Grummond, who was killed with Fetterman, left Fort Phil Kearney, accompanied by the
18th Infantry band, the latter part of January, 1867,
under orders to proceed to Fort Casper. They left
with the thermometer at 40 degrees below zero, and
with the snow so deep that they made only five miles
the first day. Several of their teamsters were badly
frozen, and one died at Fort Casper from amputation of his leg.

"This left General Wessels in command at Fort
Phil Kearney. He had nineteen sentinels posted on
and around the stockade every day and night, there
being three reliefs of the guard. Fifty-nine men
mounted guard daily, besides the officer of the day
and four non-commissioned officers.

"This large detail of men for guard duty made
it very hard on us. We often had to saw wood, for
our heating stoves in the barracks, until after tattoo
at 9 p. m.

"Through that long and terrible winter the thermometer most of the time was from 25 to 40 below
zero. We had no fresh meat and no vegetables.
One small loaf of bread was issued to us daily —
just about enough for one meal. After we had
eaten that we had to fall back on the musty hardtack and frowsy bacon or salt pork, with black
coffee. Sometimes we had bean soup. There was

THE GREAT SIOUX WAR CHIEF RED CLOUD AT 90 YEARS OF AGE,
BLIND AND INFIRM. PHOTO COURTESY OF CAPT. J. H. COOK,
AGATE, NEB.

no place in barracks where we could wash our hands and faces.*

"After the Fetterman disaster the Indians did not bother us again until spring. They had enough to do, I expect, to keep their own camps warm without molesting us, but with the coming of spring, they again started up their old tactics of the previous summer. Every time the logging parties ventured out they would be attacked. The wagon trains also were given their special attention as they came up the Bozeman Trail, scarcely a day passing without its skirmish or fierce fighting.

"We were now on the lookout for Gilmore & Porter's bull trains to come up the trail with supplies for our post, but it was well along toward June, or quite a bit after the first of that month, before they showed up. When they did come, however, they were loaded to the guards with provender.

"While this was most thankfully received, the thing that brought joy to our hearts was several hundred new improved breech-loading Springfield rifles of 50 caliber. These were the very first guns of this type ever issued to troops in the Indian country. One hundred thousand rounds of ammunition also accompanied the rifles.

"We now felt that we would stand a little better chance in our battles with the savages. The guns we had been using were antiquated muzzle-loaders, relics of the Civil War. The Indians knew this, and they also knew that once these old guns were

---

*And now, sixty years later, the U. S. Government refuses decent pensions to these brave men. Indian fighting was not recognized by the government as "War!"

fired, it took some time to reload them, and by quick charges they would accomplish considerable damage before muzzle-loading guns could be reloaded. The new guns used metallic cartridges, and it was but the work of a second, after firing, to throw open the breech-block and slap in a fresh shell. Had it not been for those breech-loaders, the Wagon Box fight, of which I am about to tell you, would have ended with our scalps dangling at the belts of Red Cloud's savage hordes.

"Gilmore & Porter's bull trains remained at the fort all summer, they having taken a contract to supply the fort with logs for the saw mill and firewood for use the following winter. Early in July a corral was constructed out some six miles from the fort. It was built with the wagon boxes taken from the logging wagons, as the running gear only was used to bring in the big logs. There were fourteen of these wagon boxes, and they were placed in the shape of a large oval. Into this corral the stock was driven nights. Here also seven thousand rounds of ammunition was kept, as well as extra rifles. It was expected that in the event of an attack, the woodchoppers and men engaged in hauling the logs would retreat to the corral and make a stand.

"Company A of our regiment had, since January 1st, been detailed to guard and do escort duty to and from the fort every day. They were also to guard the woodchoppers in the pinery. Company A was out with the train the entire month of July and only saw Indians two or three times during the month.

"On July 31st, my company (Co. C) relieved Com-

GRAVE OF RED CLOUD AT PINE RIDGE, AGENCY, SO. DAKOTA.
PHOTO COURTESY REV. FATHER GROTEGEERS.

pany A, hoping and praying we would have as easy a time from Indian attacks through August as had Company A through July. However, we were not to be let off so easily.

"The first day of August it happened that I was detailed to guard the woodchoppers at the lower pinery. For some reason or other a sense of impending danger seemed hovering in the air. The day passed quietly, however. That night I formed one of the guard around the wagon box corral, and this sense of an impending danger seemed more pronounced than ever. The night passed without any attack, although I believe — from the nature of the attack on the morning of August 2d — that Red Cloud's warriors had spent the night in surrounding our position and getting things in readiness to wipe us off the earth that morning.

"By the time the sun had risen we had finished our breakfast. Directly afterward the wagons started out — one for the fort, loaded with logs which had been brought as far as the corral the previous afternoon — and the other for the lower pinery, escorted by men enough to act as guards.

"Somewhere around seven o'clock on that 2d of August, I had instructions to relieve one of the men on picket on the banks of Little Piney Creek. Another soldier named Deming accompanied me.

"We had been there but a few minutes when there came a yell of 'Indians!' Instantly we were on the alert. Looking toward the west we observed seven or eight Indians on horseback coming across the divide on the dead run, toward our position.

"They were probably seven hundred yards away

when we discovered them. I made up my mind that here was a good chance to try some long-range shooting with my new Springfield. Dropping down behind some rocks I set my sights for what I thought was the proper distance, and let drive. As the smoke breezed away I saw the lead pony stumble and go down. I didn't get the rider, however, for he jumped up and climbed astride behind the rider in his rear.

"Glancing toward the main camp I observed some commotion there; then looking toward the foothills my hair seemed to rise right up straight, for hundreds upon hundreds of Indians were swarming down toward us. There was a woodchoppers' camp a little distance from our position, and I told Deming to run over there and warn the men. We did not dare leave our position unless signaled from the main camp, and it began to look mighty unhealthy for us, as the savages were pouring over the hills in droves.

"When Deming came back he said that the men had seen the Indians, apparently, as they had skipped out for the mountains instead of going to the corral. We now came to the conclusion that if we expected to retain our own scalps it was high time we were leaving what was getting to be a mighty unhealthy neighborhood. We decided to make a running fight of it if necessary. There were three of us guards at this point, and we at once started.

"After we had gone a few hundred yards we observed several Indians coming up out of Little Piney Creek bottom. We immediately opened fire upon

RED CLOUD AND HIS WIFE. PHOTO COURTESY OF CAPT. J. H. COOK, AGATE, NEBR. TAKEN ON THE COOK RANCH.

them. My first shot knocked a warrior off his pony.
The two other guards also began shooting at them,
as the Indians replied to our fire with whoops and
yells. They commenced coming up out of the creek
bottom in a regular swarm, like angry bees from a
hive, and it sure looked like we were not going to
reach that corral. They tried to surround us and
cut us off, but we fired so rapidly and kept up such
an incessant fusillade that they didn't dare ride in
very close to us.

"Our tongues were now hanging out and we were
about all in, but we kept on running like scared
rabbits, expecting every minute to feel a bullet or
arrow in our backs. The Indians proved to be poor
shots, however, and although their bullets kicked up
the dust around our heels, it only served to make
us run the faster.

"As we neared the corral one of the men ran out
some little distance, and dropping down on one knee
he opened a hot fire on our pursuers. Several fell
from their ponies under his steady firing. This man
proved to be a bright German named Max Littman.
I have no doubt that he saved us from being cut off
and captured.

"We were completely winded as we reeled inside
the wagon box corral. Gasping for breath I reported to Capt. James Powell the reason why we had
left our post. He commended us for our action, and
told us to hustle and find a place inside the wagon
boxes, as we would have to fight that day as we
never had fought before if we expected to save our
scalps.

"All told, our fighting force consisted of thirty-two men. The wagon boxes, I would here state, were no protection whatever from the bullets of the Indian rifles, save that they concealed us from view. They were made of inch boards, through which a rifle ball would zip as easily as though they were paper. They were not lined with boiler iron or anything else, as some writers have led the public to believe. Neither were there any loop-holes cut in them. All our fighting was done over the tops of the wagon beds, and how a man of our thirty-two escaped with his life is yet the marvel and wonder of everybody who has ever read of this extraordinary engagement.

"I was the youngest member of the party, being but 18 years of age, and I knew — as one soldier remarked to me — that I would 'have to fight like hell today.' Ammunition boxes were being hurriedly opened and their contents distributed, and I carried a hundred rounds of the big 50-caliber shells to my place in the wagon box where I had been delegated to fight. Captain Powell was giving orders rapidly and coolly. One look at the faces of those thirty-two men convinced me that we were up against it good and proper, and that we had got to fight like demons if we saved our hair. None of us had the least idea that we would come out of the battle alive. Red Cloud had three thousand of his choicest braves arrayed against us that hot summer day, and what could thirty-two men do against such an army, even though they were armed with breech-loading rifles?

"But the Indians had not reckoned on one thing. They knew nothing of our new rifles, and supposed

CHIEF RED CLOUD, LEADER OF THE SIOUX IN THE WAGON BOX
FIGHT, WHOSE WARRIORS WERE THE SCOURGE OF THE PLAINS
IN 1866. BORN 1824, DIED 1910, AT PINE RIDGE RESERVATION,
SO. DAKOTA. FROM A COPYRIGHTED PHOTO BY MAJOR GEORGE
INGALLS. TAKEN ABOUT 1876.

we were yet armed only with muzzle-loading weapons, and that all they had to do was to let us fire
once, and then charge us and wipe us out before
we could reload. Those new Springfield breech-
loaders saved the day for us.

"After I had deposited my ammunition in a handy
place I joined a group of men who were watching
the Indians advancing toward our position. There
was no laughing or joking. Every man's face bore
a look of grim determination. Some of them were
hastily piling up various articles behind which to
do battle. Others were wheeling barrels and boxes
into position, preferring to fight behind them rather
than inside the wagon boxes. One man knelt behind a barrel of beans; another chose a barrel of salt
as his barricade. Others were engaged in attaching
strings to the triggers of their rifles. I knew what
this meant — those men never would be captured
alive. They would save the last shot for themselves
by fitting the loop of the string over their boot,
placing the muzzle of the rifle against their own
heads and springing the trigger. However, it never
became necessary to resort to this last desperate
measure.

"Lieut. Jenness was watching a big bunch of the
Indians down the Big Piney valley, and others on
the ridges east of our position. All were bearing
down toward the corral, and we were immediately
ordered inside the wagon boxes. The last and only
command given during the entire fight by Captain
Powell was, 'Men, here they come! Get your places
and shoot to kill!'

"Immediately our little band opened the ball. A

crashing volley shot out from the wagon boxes, and as the exultant savages dashed forward, expecting they had us at their mercy, they were met with another staggering fire, which mowed them down and opened great gaps in their ranks. Breaking, they dropped back apparently in consternation. They could not understand the rapidity of our fire, and doubtless thought we had more men in our party than they had been led to believe.

"Out in front of us the plain was strewn with dead and dying Indians and kicking, screaming ponies. They could not stand up before such shooting, and they withdrew some distance, where their leaders appeared to be holding a consultation. We could see that we had damaged them considerably with our first volleys, and our hopes began to rise.

"Presently we observed a large body of the savages signaling with pocket mirrors toward the ridge to the east of us. We afterward learned that these signals were seen and understood by Indians many miles away. Apparently they had a reserve force which they were calling into action. Suddenly someone on the north side of the corral yelled, 'Look out! they're coming again!' and we prepared for another desperate charge.

"We had forgotten — or neglected — to pull down several tents which formed part of our camp equipage, and these were somewhat obstructing our view. Two men accordingly leaped out and ran swiftly toward them and began pulling them down. Johnny Grady, sitting alongside me, yelled, 'Come on, kid, let's have a hand in that.' We jumped out and loosened the ropes around the tent pins until

OLD FORT LARAMIE AS IT LOOKED IN 1902, YEARS AFTER ITS ABANDONMENT BY THE GOVERNMENT AS AN ARMY POST.   PHOTO BY HON. JOHN HUNTON.

(68)

all but one of the tents had fallen. The Indians were now so close that we had to abandon the last one and rush back to resume fighting.

"We had a much better view of the field with the tents out of the way, and again opened a most galling and rapid fire upon the advancing hordes. It was almost impossible to miss getting an Indian at every shot, as they were so close. If they had possessed the military genius to charge us, or had had plenty of horsemen behind their foot-fighters to do so, we could not possibly have lasted five minutes. Again we opened great gaps in their ranks, and once more they drew off out of range.

"During this momentary lull word was passed around that Lieut. Jenness had been killed, as well as Privates Haggerty and Tommy Doyle — the latter being the man I had observed piling up the neck yokes to fight behind.

"We had neglected to bring any water inside the wagon boxes with us. It was a terribly hot day, and we now began to suffer from thirst. There was a barrel half filled with water about twenty feet outside the corral where the cooks had been preparing the meals. This had been repeatedly struck by bullets and the water had nearly all leaked out. There was one wagon near the west end of the corral, and under this the cook had placed two camp kettles in which coffee had been made that morning. The cook had afterward filled them with water on top of the old coffee grounds, intending to use it for the company supper.

"We now planned to secure those camp kettles. Johnny Grady said he would go, and asked me to

THE COBBLESTONE MONUMENT ON "MASSACRE HILL", ERECTED
BY THE STATE OF WYOMING TO FETTERMAN DISASTER VICTIMS.
PHOTO BY E. A. BRININSTOOL.

accompany him. We crawled out of our wagon box, and on our stomachs commenced hitching along toward the coveted kettles, hugging the ground as closely as possible. We were apparently not observed and this gave us confidence. Reaching the kettles we each grabbed one and began crawling back. Just then came several sputtering shots and 'z-z-zip! p-i-n-g!' and bullets struck the kettles, but we got back in time to save most of the water — dirty, black stuff, but a God-send nevertheless.

"And now came the big charge of the day! A cry from the west end of the corral drew our attention that way, and we saw a sight that chilled our blood. Hundreds upon hundreds of the savages were swarming up out of a ravine not over ninety yards from the west end of the corral. Their numbers appeared to be unlimited. All were on foot, formed in the shape of a big V or wedge. We at once sent several crashing volleys into the mass. Scores fell, but others filled the gaps. On they came until they were so close that we could see the whites of their eyes, and the heavy balls from our rifles must have pierced two or three bodies. They did not waver or falter until almost upon us, and just as it looked as if we must be overpowered, they suddenly broke and fled in consternation and disorder, leaving scores of their dead and wounded behind. Several hundred mounted warriors were on the plain to the south, closely watching this foot charge. Had these Indians but possessed the military genius to have backed up this foot charge with a determined mounted charge, they would have wiped us out in the shake of a buck's tail.

"We had been fighting since seven o'clock in the morning and it was now after three in the afternoon. All this time we were wondering if the fighting had been heard at the fort and if a relief party would come to our aid. After the last desperate charge of the enemy we observed several leaving the scene of the conflict, going down a steep incline into the Big Pine valley. We did not understand this move, but considered they were hatching up some new form of deviltry.

"Suddenly we distinctly heard the boom of a big gun to the east of us. We quickly recognized it as one of the howitzers from the fort. The relief was approaching! The Indians on the plain in front of us also were slipping away. A long line of blue presently appeared. It was the advance skirmishers, and maybe those old blue uniforms didn't look good to us! Most of our men acted like maniacs at the sight of them — could not believe that they were at last saved from destruction — they leaped to their feet, whooping and yelling; they sobbed and cried, hugged each other and danced about in a perfect delirium of delight that the terrible strain was over and we were now safe.

"Major Smith was in command of the relief party. He had brought along Dr. Horton, the post surgeon. They had not expected to find a man of us alive. The genial doctor had thoughtfully brought along a small keg of whiskey, and the first thing he did was to give every man a drink.

"We now took stock of our condition. We had lost three men killed and several were badly wounded. The tops of those wagon boxes were ripped to slivers,

CAPTAIN FREDERICK BROWN.   KILLED IN THE FETTERMAN
DISASTER.

but our losses were slight in comparison to those
of the Indians. On the way back to the fort, as we
topped a big rise of ground, we halted and looked
back up Big Pine valley. Here we saw an immense
number of Indian ponies, three and four deep, dragging travois loaded with dead and wounded Indians.

"It is impossible to tell the exact number of Indians killed in this extraordinary engagement.
Many years ago, at Pine Ridge reservation, where
Chief Red Cloud passed his declining years, he stated
that he went into that fight with three thousand of
his choicest fighting warriors and came out with but
half of them! This seems incredible. The men of
my company estimated that several hundred must
have been killed and wounded. In 1895, at Standing
Rock reservation, Chief Rain-in-the-Face told me,
through an interpreter, that he did not care to dis-
cuss the wagon box fight.

"After our battle of August 2d, the Indians kept
up their harassing operations by attacking citizen
bull trains going up the Bozeman Trail to Fort C. F.
Smith on the Big Horn river, and our company was
surrounded and attacked by hostiles on Peno Creek,
about November 11th, some eight or nine miles
north of Fort Phil Kearney. They ran off seven
head of our cattle, but we got the balance inside our
corral, and gave these Indians another good licking,
after which they did not again bother us until spring
came. Then General Sherman came up to Fort Phil
Kearney with some more Peace Commissioners in
May, and with Red Cloud and other noted chiefs a
treaty was formulated.

"Red Cloud stipulated that the Indians should be

given back their hunting grounds, including all the territory north of Fort Fetterman, on the banks of the North Platte river, as far north as the Gallatin Valley in Montana. Further, that all the forts which Col. Carrington had established should be abandoned and the troops withdrawn from the country. Red Cloud would consider no other proposition whatever, and the Commissioners were obliged to come to his terms.

"We evacuated Fort Phil Kearney early in August, 1868, and I was one of the soldiers who marched out from the historic old post, the scene of more Indian fights than any other fort ever erected in the entire western country. Even before we were out of sight of the post, the Indians swarmed out of the adjacent ravines and fired the buildings.

"We arrived at Fort D. A. Russell, near Cheyenne, Wyoming, some three weeks later, back to civilization, and mighty glad to sample potatoes, cabbage and other vegetables, not having tasted anything of the kind for months.

"My company was detailed to guard the Union Pacific railroad from Plum Creek, Nebraska, east to Kearney Station, until some time in November. Our company was then ordered to Fort Kearney, Nebraska, on the south side of the Platte river, to relieve Light Battery C, 3d Artillery (Sinclair's Battery), and we took station there. As soon as we got into barracks a general 'delousing' took place in the company, and we could then sleep a little more in comfort.

"We remained at Fort Kearney during the winter of 1868-'69, and I was discharged on the 11th of

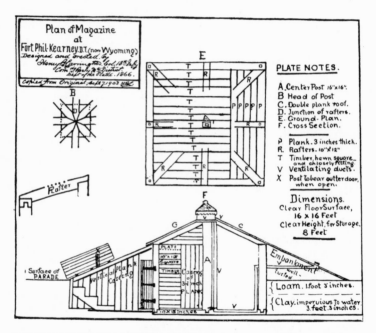

BUILDING PLAN OF FORT PHIL KEARNEY, WYOMING, 1866.   DRAWN
BY COL. H. B. CARRINGTON.

April following. However, I enlisted again. All told I served forty-eight years in the regular army and passed through many other Indian campaigns; but my nerves never were put to the severe test they experienced on that 2d of August, 1867, when we fought Red Cloud's braves from the Wagon Box corral."

EAST LINE OF THE STOCKADE OF OLD FORT PHIL KEARNEY—NOTE SECTION OF LOG JUST BELOW WIRE FENCE. PHOTO BY E. A. BRININSTOOL.

CHAPTER III

THE "ISLAND OF DEATH"

HOW FORSYTH'S SCOUTS FOUGHT THE CHEYENNES AT BEECHER ISLAND.

NOTE — The battle of Beecher Island, fought September 17, 1868, between 51 frontier scouts and more than 700 Northern Cheyenne Indians, on the Arickaree Fork of the Republican River, in the extreme eastern portion of the present state of Colorado, is conceded by old frontiersmen and army officers to have been one of the most desperate and extraordinary engagements between white men and Indians in all the annals of Indian warfare in the West. Mr. Sigmund Shlesinger, today a retired merchant of Cleveland, Ohio, and a friend of the author, who, in 1868, as a mere boy of 17, (the youngest member of Forsyth's Scouts), took an active part in the battle, here recounts his experiences in this desperate defence. — E. A. BRININSTOOL.

"TO relate my experiences while a member of Forsyth's Scouts during the fight with Indians on Beecher Island, September 17, 1868, I am obliged to anticipate that thrilling event with a statement as to how I happened to be on the Plains, and the incidents which led up to my enlisting in Col. Geo. A. Forsyth's detachment of Indian fighters, with a brief summary of the events which started us on the warpath against the Indian tribes which were devastating the frontier settlements of western Kansas at that time.

(78)

"At my home in New York City, in 1865, I was engaged by a merchant of Leavenworth, Kansas, and taken by him to his western home. I remained in his employ as clerk for over a year. At this time the Union Pacific Railroad was being built across the Plains. The end of track reached Junction City, or Fort Riley, when rumors of fruitful trading with the railroad workers and military guarding the workers influenced me to join the throngs drifting toward the frontier along the surveyed line of proposed track. From Junction City we traveled to a settlement called Salina. When I reached this place the citizens were preparing to defend the town against a threatened Indian attack, but the rumors seem to have been a false alarm.

"From here, after a time, I moved with the tide along the grading of the proposed railroad. This was a new country. Towns sprang up over night. Communities moved houses and effects in a few days to any locality that seemed promising to become the 'end of the track,' and a prospect for trade with the railroad employes.

"I found work of various kinds and nature. I was clerk in a clothing store, barkeeper in a tent liquor house, waiter in a tent hotel, clerk in a grocery, shoveled on the railroad, cooked for a mess of teamsters, night-herded mules for a contractor and drove mules hauling stone from a quarry. In this latter experience I had my first Indian scare. I obtained this job of mule driving from Contractor Fish at Fort Hays, because he wanted me to vote for him in an election, the nature of which I did not understand, but I voted as directed.

S. SHLESINGER, THE YOUNGEST MEMBER OF "FORSYTH'S SCOUTS."
NOW LIVING IN CLEVELAND, OHIO.

"One day I was ordered with my team to take some wood-choppers to Big Creek, about twelve miles east of Fort Hays. At the time there was no general outbreak of Indians, but occasionally rumors reached the settlements of small bands attacking travelers or isolated settlers, evidently bent on pilfering. No general alarm was felt. My party had guns and revolvers, but were not provided with ammunition. I was driving alongside the railroad up an incline, nearing our destination, at some distance the other side of the summit, where a troop of cavalry was stationed to guard this portion of the track-workers. In my wagon box were seated the woodchoppers, who were talking and joking. One of the men was sitting on a hard-tack box, and thereby had a higher view of the surrounding country.

"All at once he called our attention to some moving objects several miles distant. It was not very long until we could discern that those objects were mounted Indians, coming our way at a rapid gait. Needless to say, the scare nearly paralyzed my senses, and I was impelled to lay the whip on the backs of my mules in no gentle manner. We soon reached the top of the incline, the Indians — about half a dozen of them — coming along swiftly. We here started down the grade toward Big Creek, yelling with all our might to attract the attention of the soldiers. When we were about half-way down the incline the Indians reached the top of the grade and commenced shooting at us, their few bullets kicking up the dust as they struck the ground around us; but the soldiers, being attracted by our commotion, quickly mounted and came at full tilt toward us. The Indians moved off leisurely, and we watched them disappear around the bluffs.

"The day I arrived at Fort Hays most of the townspeople were out on the prairie watching William F. Cody (Buffalo Bill) chase a buffalo and bring the animal down with his rifle. From this carcass I had my first taste of buffalo meat.

"That winter I peddled papers among the soldiers of the Seventh and Tenth Cavalry. Gen. George Custer was one of my customers, as was "Wild Bill" Hickok, the noted scout. In my varied duties I became acquainted with many of the government scouts at Fort Hays and other posts, whom I sometimes accompanied on their trips carrying dispatches between military posts and camps.

"In the summer of 1868 I became entirely out of funds, living on hardtack and coffee most of the time, going from camp to camp looking for something to do. About this time Col. George A. Forsyth was organizing a company of frontier men to scout for Indian warfare. The Cheyennes had taken to the warpath and were sweeping through western Kansas like a whirlwind of death. In a single month they killed or captured eighty-four settlers and their wives and children. They burnt, destroyed and laid waste everything in their path.

"It was in the midst of this excitement that I eagerly sought an engagement with Forsyth's Scouts. I succeeded through the influence of C. W. Parr, post scout at Fort Hays. His interest in my obtaining membership in the command was due to the fact that the pay of the Scouts, who had their

BEECHER ISLAND BATTLEGROUND (LOOKING UP THE ARICKAREE)
PHOTO BY E. A. BRININSTOOL.

own horses, was to be $75 per month, while those
who drew horses from the government were to receive $50.   Parr loaned several of his horses to a
few of the men, myself among the number, for
which he drew $25 per month of our pay.

"Although I had had no military experience, I
was fairly well inured to prairie life, acquired by
my two years of knocking about on the frontier, so
that the prospects of this campaign did not deter
me from entering cheerfully upon the expected adventure — perhaps because I did not know what was
coming.

"Forsyth's company of Scouts was commanded
by himself, while Lieut. Fred Beecher — a nephew
of Henry Ward Beecher, the world-famous divine —
was detailed as second in command.   Our surgeon
was a Dr. John H. Mooers, a physician who had settled at Fort Hays, and was familiar with frontier
life.   The guide of the expedition was Sharp Grover,
one of the most reliable plainsmen of those times.
We were equipped with saddle, bridle, haversack,
canteen, blanket, knife, tin cup, a Spencer repeating
rifle and a heavy Colt revolver.   Four mules constituted our baggage train, but we carried no tents
or like equipage.

"When we left Fort Hays upon our first scout
— our full complement being fifty-one men — we
started in a northwesterly direction.   We traveled
all day, save for a short rest for lunch, and did not
go into camp until we reached the Salina River, late
that night. I will never forget the first day's ride. I
was not familiar to the saddle, and my equipment
was all the time where it should not have been.   My

bridle arm became stiff; my equipment would not
remain in any one place, and I was sore and galled.
I was too exhausted to eat any supper, while to cap
the climax, I was detailed for guard duty.   But
human nature could stand the strain no longer, and
no sooner was I directed to my post than I dropped
on the ground and fell fast asleep.   Had there been
thousands of Indians around us, my condition could
not have prevented them from making an assault.
But it did not take many days for me to become
hardened and fit for any emergency.

"After a short scout without discovering anything
of marauding Indians, we arrived at Fort Wallace.
While here, word came in that a Mexican wagon
train had been attacked near the settlement of Sheridan.   We lost the trail of the Indians after scouting
around Sheridan, and we then continued on into the
northern country, where there was no road or trail.

"For several days we scouted about, scanning remains of old or recent campfires, hunting buffalo
and antelope for food, but otherwise without incident, until finally our flankers reported finding a
sign of a trail.   This we took and followed.   Other
trails began to lead into this one, until finally it became so broad and distinct that there was no longer
any doubt of our having struck the trail of a large
war party.   Those who were experienced Indian
fighters told us that we must be following the track
of an Indian village on the move, with a large herd
of horses.   Remarks as to possibilities regarding the
probable number of the Indians, when or how we
would come in contact with them, and the possible
result, were subjects under discussion.   Some of the

JOHN HURST, ONE OF "FORSYTH'S SCOUTS." PHOTO BY E. A.
BRININSTOOL IN 1917.   MR. HURST HAS SINCE PASSED AWAY.

more experienced made predictions to which I, at least — the most inexperienced and youngest of the command — gave attentive ear, and everybody was tense with excitement.   Game was no longer about us — a sure sign that Indians were in advance of us, and our meals became very circumscribed.

"On the afternoon of September 16th, as our horses were jaded from long and hard riding, Col. Forsyth decided to camp on a spot that looked inviting as regards good grazing.   It was much earlier in the day than we had been in the habit of stopping for our night camp.   This circumstance alone undoubtedly proved to be an act of Providence.   Had we traveled but half a mile further we would have fallen into an ambush most ingeniously prepared, and the scheme so favored by topographical formation of the country, that had we passed that way, not a mother's son of us would probably have escaped alive!   But we were ignorant of the fact at the time.

"We went into camp in a valley some two miles wide and about the same in length.   Through this valley ran a small stream known as the Arickaree fork of the Republican River, and our command encamped on the south bank about four o'clock in the afternoon.   We were opposite a flat plateau which formed a small island by the overflow of the stream in flood season.   At this time of the year, however, but a few inches of water was flowing in the bed of the stream, which divided at the upper end of the tiny island and meandered slowly by on each side, until it again entered the main stream perhaps a hundred yards below.   The width of this island was about twenty yards. A solitary cotton-wood tree was growing at the lower end and the island itself was covered with a growth of stunted bushes, principally alders and willows.

"Sentries were posted and there was no alarm during the night, but just before daybreak Col. Forsyth, who had kept a vigilant watch during most of the night, happened to be standing by one of the sentries.   Silhouetted against the skyline both discerned the feathered head-dress of an Indian.   The crack of a rifle was echoed by whoops from a party of Indians who dashed out toward the horse herd, rattling bells, dry hides, buffalo skins and other devices calculated to stampede the mounts of our command.   None but the pack animals were lost, however, but these carried all the medical supplies, for lack of which the entire command suffered severely later.

"At the first fire every man of us sprang to our feet.   There was a sharp exchange of shots, and the little band of savages were driven away.   We were ordered to saddle up instantly, and stand ready for action.   Scarcely were we thus assembled when Grover, the guide, uttered an exclamation of alarm, and pointed down the valley.

" 'My God!' he cried, 'look at the Injuns!'

"In front of us, to our right, in our rear, the hills and valleys were suddenly transformed from peace and quiet to a scene filled with hundreds upon hundreds of mounted and unmounted warriors. They seemed to spring from the ground like Roderick Dhu's Highland Scots. Out from the tall grass across the slope on the south, came Indians in

THE FIRST NIGHT STILLWELL AND TRUDEAU CRAWLING OUT ON HANDS AND KNEES, STARTED FOR RELIEF, AND HIDING DAYS AND TRAVELING NIGHTS, REACHED FT. WALLACE.

THE THIRD NIGHT, DONOVAN AND PLILEY STARTED, ARRIVING AT THE FORT. DONOVAN WITH FOUR OTHERS IMMEDIATELY STARTED BACK, AND COMING UPON COL. CARPENTER'S COMMAND, ON THE SOUTH FORK OF THE REPUBLICAN, GUIDED THEM IN A TWENTY MILE DASH, REACHING THE ISLAND AT 10 A.M. THE NINTH DAY, 26 HOURS IN ADVANCE OF COL. BANKHEAD, WITH SCOUTS STILLWELL AND TRUDEAU.

THE RETURN TO FT. WALLACE WAS BEGUN SEPT. 27 TH. THE WOUNDED BEING CARRIED IN GOVERNMENT WAGONS.

INSCRIPTION ON SOUTH SIDE OF BEECHER ISLAND BATTLE MONU-
MENT. PHOTO BY E. A. BRININSTOOL.

hordes! It was a sight which but few men have been permitted to look upon and live to tell about.

"I will frankly admit that I was frightened almost out of my senses. I felt as if I wanted to run somewhere, but every avenue of escape seemed closed. Look where I might, only death faced me, and death in its most hideous and awful form; so I naturally turned to Col. Forsyth as my protector, as a young chick flutters to its mother's wings in time of danger. I was reassured by his remarkable coolness and self-possession.

"Someone — I think it was young Jack Stillwell — at once suggested the little island as our only avenue of defense. Apparently the Indians had forgotten to occupy it in their endeavor to surround and cut us off, as there was no movement by them to take possession of it. Col. Forsyth at once gave orders to move to the island. I was just behind the Colonel when the first volley was fired at us by our foes. However, we gained the island without the loss of a single man or horse. Here we immediately tied our animals to the bushes, although we well knew they would soon be shot down to prevent any escapes in that way.

"We were outnumbered more than twenty to one, yet we immediately prepared to sell our lives as dearly as possible. We placed ourselves in a position lying flat on the ground, and at once drew our knives and began to prepare a barricade by scooping out the sand and piling it before us. By kicking with our heels and toes into the soft earth we soon had holes deep enough to offer fairly good protection.

"The Indians were plainly filled with disgust at

their failure to take possession of the island, in which event we would have been completely at their mercy. We could see their chiefs riding furiously about and, with more military skill than one would credit them with, they began deliberate preparations for battle.

"Sharp Grover passed around word that the Indians were the Northern Cheyennes, under a famous chief named "Roman Nose," allied with some of the Ogallala and Brule Sioux, and a few "Dog Soldiers" (renegade Cheyennes). They were accompanied by their squaws and children, who took positions on a high bluff overlooking the battlefield, but just out of range, where they could watch their husbands and brothers "clean up" the hated white despoilers of their land. This bluff is now known as "Squaw Hill."

"It was not long before we were assailed by a perfect storm of rifle bullets. The Indians, after showing off in massed formation, began circling around us, displaying such magnificent horsemanship as I have never seen before or since. Rifle smoke and clouds of dust, shot through with flashes of powder, are ever in my memory when I think of that awful fight. They charged us repeatedly, but with our seven-shot Spencer carbines we were enabled to withstand every charge, so that the enemy broke and passed our little defense on both sides without once gaining a foothold on the island. With every repulse they seemed to gain new acquisitions and strength. Every once in awhile a cry would go up from our boys that this one or that one was hit,

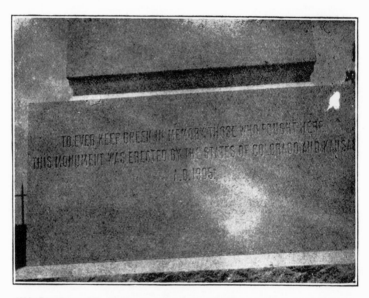

INSCRIPTION ON BASE OF BEECHER ISLAND BATTLE MONUMENT.
PHOTO BY E. A. BRININSTOOL.

and that Scouts Wilson and Culver had been killed. Our horses, of course, were soon all shot down.

"Col. Forsyth received a bullet through the thigh and another crashed through his knee, while a third passed so close to his head as to cause a slight scalp wound. Dr. Mooers was struck in the forehead at the very beginning of the fight, and never spoke again, although he lived three days. Lieut. Beecher was mortally wounded. He dragged himself to Col. Forsyth's side and made him acquainted with the nature of his wound, then bidding his commander goodbye, our brave lieutenant laid down with his head upon his arm and soon passed away.

"The Indian loss during the first day's siege was severe, although I do not know to what extent. During the night they removed their dead, so we had no way of ascertaining their exact loss. However, when night threw her welcome shade about us, and we had time to take account of our own condition, it was found that seven or eight of our men were dead or supposed to be dying, and sixteen others suffered wounds of one kind or another. As for myself, I still remained unhurt, although I had kept my rifle redhot all day long.

"At dark the Indians withdrew and then Nature began to assert itself. I was hungry, but there was nothing to eat. I recalled that in my saddlebags were some wild plums which I had gathered the day before. I got out of my hole, and creeping on hands and knees to the spot where my dead horse lay, began feeling about in the darkness. I came in contact with something cold, and upon examination found it was Scout Wilson's pallid hand! He had been killed some time during the first charges. The shivers chased up and down my back, but I got to my horse and tugged until I secured the saddlebags containing the plums.

"We were in a desperate condition. The nearest point from which relief might be had was Fort Wallace, about 125 miles distant. However, the relief could not be expected unless some one from among us could crawl through the Indian cordon drawn about us and reach the fort with news of our plight. As soon as darkness had fully settled down, Col. Forsyth held a council. His own condition was precarious. He went over the situation, and then called for volunteers for the dangerous journey. It was about one chance in a thousand that anyone could get through the Indian lines, which we knew would be still more closely drawn through the night to guard against just such an attempt. But there were men among us who did not falter.

"Young Jack Stillwell, a beardless boy of but nineteen, but a man in cool, daring bravery and frontier skill, was the first to offer his services. Pierre Trudeau, an old plainsman and trapper, agreed to go with Jack. Their plans were quickly made. With a note from Col. Forsyth, explaining the dangerous condition of the Scouts, the two men crawled out through the darkness. We listened for some time, fully expecting every moment to hear the warwhoop which would announce their discovery and capture, but not a sound followed their departure. I will say here that the men were successful in their undertaking, although they underwent many thrilling and hairbreath escapes before they

JACK STILLWELL, OF "FORSYTH'S SCOUTS."

(95)

reached Fort Wallace, of which I have not space to tell.

"The following day was a repetition of the first. The Indians attacked us again at daylight, but there were fewer casualties among us, due to the fact that during the night we had strengthened and dug deeper in our rifle pits. We had also been enabled to dig down to water, being so close to the stream, so that we had plenty to drink and to bathe the wounds of our comrades. But there was not a morsel of food for us unless we chose to make use of the dead horses lying about us. This, Col. Forsyth urged us to take advantage of, so large quantities of horsemeat were cut and buried deep in the cool sand, where it would keep sweet longer, while yet more was cooked over fires in our pits, for immediate consumption. This work was all done on the first night following the attack.

"The weather throughout the daytime was insufferably hot, and the second day of the siege closed with the Indians still hemming us in as closely as ever. It looked as though they were determined to starve us out, and it certainly seemed to me that their plans were going to be realized. That night two more of our men, Allison Pliley and a scout by the name of Donovan, with a note to the commanding officer at Fort Wallace, also started out. We had no way of knowing, of course, whether Stillwell and Trudeau would reach the fort. These men (Pliley and Donovan) met Col. Carpenter, of the Tenth Cavalry, on the second or third day of their departure, while he was out on a scout, and Carpenter was the first to reach us. That was on the ninth day after the attack.

"The third day was a repetition of the first two, although the Indians did not attack us with the same persistence and determination, but they made it hot enough for us, so that we were compelled to hug our defenses mighty closely. By this time the horse meat was becoming putrid and terribly offensive. We tried sprinkling gunpowder over it, but it did little good. An unlucky coyote wandered over onto the island that day, and one of the men succeeded in shooting it. However, it did not go very far among so many men. The wounded were now suffering agonies, and to add to their misery, gangrene set in, and their wounds became festered and in terrible condition. We had no way whatever of relieving their suffering, save by the application of cold water bandages.

"To make this story short, for nine days we were in a state of siege, yet never for a moment did our brave leader lose heart or think of giving up the fight. The suffering of all the uninjured men was terrible, but that of the wounded pitiful and excruciating. On the ninth day the Indians had nearly all withdrawn, as it seemed plain to them that they could not capture our position nor drive us out onto the open plain. Had they stuck to it and driven their charges home about the third or fourth day, I fear we would not have been able to withstand their assaults, as we were too weak from loss of food and sleep.

"I have often been asked whether I killed any Indians in this fight of my own knowledge. I must

GRAVE OF LIEUT. F. H. BEECHER FOR WHOM "BEECHER ISLAND"
WAS NAMED. PHOTO BY E. A. BRININSTOOL.

answer truthfully that I do not know. The conditions were such — speaking for myself — that I did not consider it safe to watch the result of a shot, the Indians being all about us, shooting at everything moving above ground. At one time I threw a hatful of sand that I scraped up in my pit to the top of the excavation, exposing myself more than usual, when a perfect hail of bullets struck my hill of sand, almost blinding me! This will explain why I did not look around for results! My plan of observation was to work the barrel of my rifle, saw fashion, through the sand, obtaining in this manner a sort of loophole through which I could see for quite a distance. In such instances I saw Indians crawl behind a knoll and drag a body away between them. I saw Indians shooting arrows at us, and bodies of savages both on foot and horseback, charging toward us. These I considered targets.

"In only one instance do I suspect of having done personal execution. In the south channel of the stream was a tree trunk, evidently brought there by the flood waters. From this tree trunk came many shots, to the great annoyance of the scout who occupied the pit with me, as well as to my own discomfiture. Finally, the scout was wounded. I did a little "sniping" in that direction, and presently no more shots came from behind that tree trunk!

"It was on the ninth day when Col. Carpenter reached us. By that time most of the Indians had departed, but we did not dare leave our position with the wounded in such awful condition. I cannot describe the joy with which we greeted Carpenter's command after facing death so many days. It was like getting a new lease on life.

"Our command was at once moved back about half a mile from the island, where we remained for two or three days while the wounded were being put in shape to stand the long journey to Fort Wallace. The rescuers delighted in feeding us with the best they had, and this kindness was continued all the way to the fort.

"At one place where we camped for the night we discovered an Indian burial pyre. There was a mound of stones piled up around the body — evidently a warrior killed in the battle with us. We also found scaffolds upon which were bodies of dead Indians. All the corpses were pulled down by our scouts for examination. This may seem like wanton sacrilege, but not to those who have suffered bodily torture and mental anguish from these same tribes. I had no scruples against rolling one of the dead Indians from his blanket. This particular one was wearing a head-dress or war bonnet made of buckskin, beautifully beaded and ornamented, with polished buffalo horns on the sides and eagle feathers down the back. Maggots were in the headpiece when I removed it. I also got the savage's beaded knife scabbard and a few other trinkets. One of the blankets the corpse was wrapped in, one earring and the knife scabbard are yet in my possession. But I had great trouble to carry these articles along, owing to the awful stench. No one would tolerate me near. When I was ready to mount I tied the bundle to the saddle girth under the animal's body, and when I rode in a wagon I tied it to an axle.

BEECHER ISLAND BATTLE MONUMENT. ERECTED BY THE STATES OF COLORADO AND KANSAS, AT A COST OF $5,000. PHOTO BY E. A. BRININSTOOL.

When we reached Fort Wallace I at once soaked my trophies in the creek, weighting them down with stones. Here my war bonnet was an object of great curiosity. One of the officers offered me $50 for it, but I refused to part with it. Next morning it was missing from my tent, and I never saw it again.

"Col. Forsyth, of course, could not assume further command of the organization, so new recruits were added, and Lieut. Papoon was installed as our new leader. I remained with the command, and was out on two more scouts with it, but nothing of importance occurred, so I resigned, and at the earnest solicitation of my family, I returned to my former home in New York City. Later, I removed to Cleveland, Ohio, where I have since been engaged in business.

"And now comes a curious aftermath of the Beecher Island fight. William F. Cody, who had obtained the sobriquet of Buffalo Bill since I had known him at Fort Hays, and who often called upon me in Cleveland when his Wild West show was performing there, invited me to visit the show grounds on one occasion. I did so, and while looking about I came across a typical-looking old plainsman who seemed to me to be the real thing. I approached him and asked:

" 'Did you live in Kansas in 1868, and if so, did you know any of Forsyth's Scouts?'

" 'Wal, I reckon I was there and knowed 'em. I was with Col. Carpenter when he rescued Forsyth,' he replied.

"I then made myself known to him as a former member of Forsyth's command, and the man —

whose name was John Y. Nelson — asked me to go to his tent over in the Indian encampment. Arriving there, we entered his tepee. Here, sitting on a buffalo robe, was an old squaw, surrounded by pappooses. Nelson said she was his wife. He said something to her in the Indian tongue, whereupon she looked up at me quickly, grunted, then arose and grasped my hand. Although this manifestation seemed friendly, I became somewhat scared, as the old squaw continued her chatter. I then asked Nelson what she was saying.

" 'This Injun is a Cheyenne,' was his reply, 'and she says she is glad to see you. The day of the attack on Forsyth's men she was one of the women who stood on the hill, just out of rifle shot, and watched the fight.'

"The old squaw then asked me, through Nelson, which one of Forsyth's men had worn a buckskin shirt. I reflected a moment, and then remembered that Jack Stillwell brought such a garment to camp before we started from Fort Hays. I helped him sew a seam around the collar. I told Nelson that Stillwell wore a buckskin shirt, wondering what the inquiry meant, and asked the reason thereof. Nelson replied:

" 'Do you remember the three dead Injuns your people scalped on the edge of the island where those Injuns were shot? Wal, one of 'em was a relative of my wife, and she says it was a man in a buckskin shirt that did the scalping.'

"Nelson and his wife further told me that the Indian loss in the fight was about seventy-five killed and many others wounded."

SITE OF THE BATTLE OF BEECHER ISLAND, SEPT. 17, 1868, ON
THE ARICKAREE FORK OF THE REPUBLICAN RIVER, EASTERN
COLORADO. PHOTO BY E. A. BRININSTOOL.

At this late day there are but a handful of Forsyth's Scouts living. The battlefield on the Arickaree is sacred and hallowed ground. The government has made it a national park. Every year on September 17th is held a reunion of the survivors, augmented by thousands from near-by towns and villages. No longer does the little island exist. The shifting sands of the Arickaree have closed the south channel of the stream, and cattle stand knee-deep in the shallow waters, while near at hand is a simple white shaft, erected by the states of Kansas and Colorado, telling the story of Forsyth's defense of the little island which was named in honor of brave Lieut. Fred Beecher, who gave his life on that occasion. Congress has set aside 120 acres of land on this site. The exact location of the battleground is in Yuma County, Colorado, fifteen miles from the thriving little city of Wray, on the Burlington Railroad.

CHAPTER IV

THE BUFFALO WALLOW FIGHT

HONORS FOR SCOUT BILLY DIXON AFTER FIFTY YEARS.

ONE of the most thrilling experiences, combined with desperate fighting, in the annals of frontier history, in which four enlisted soldiers and two army scouts successfully withstood for an entire day, the combined attack of about one hundred and twenty-five Kiowa and Comanche Indians, occurred on September 12, 1874, in an old buffalo wallow near the Washita River, in what today is Hemphill county, Texas, twenty-two miles south of the present town of Canadian, and twenty-five miles southeast of Miami. In 1874 this section was a wilderness, practically as unknown as the heart of Africa. These men were carrying dispatches from the camp of Gen. Nelson A. Miles, on McClellan Creek, in the Texas Panhandle, to Camp Supply, Indian Territory.

In order that the reader may, at the beginning, intelligently understand the situation, the author appends herewith the official report of General Miles, relative to the affair:

"HEADQUARTERS INDIAN TERRITORY EXPEDITION
Camp on Washita River, Texas,
Sept. 24, 1874.
"ADJUTANT GENERAL, U. S. A.
(Through Office Asst. Adj. Gen. Hdqtrs.
Dept. and Mil. District of the Missouri, and
of the Army.)

"GENERAL:

"I deem it but a duty to brave and heroic men and faithful soldiers, to bring to the notice of the highest military authorities, an instance of indomitable courage, skill and true heroism on the part of a detachment from this command with the request that the actors may be rewarded and their faithfulness and bravery recognized, by pensions, Medals of Honor, or in such way as may be deemed most fitting.

"On the night of the 10th inst., a party consisting of Sergt. Z. T. Woodall, Co. I; Privates Peter Rath, Co. A; John Harrington, Co. H, and George W. Smith, Co. M, Sixth Cavalry, and Scouts Amos Chapman and William Dixon, were sent as bearers of dispatches from the camp of this command on McClellan Creek to Camp Supply, I. T.

"At 6 a. m. on the 12th, when approaching the Washita River, they were met and surrounded by a band of about one hundred and twenty-five Kiowas and Comanches, who had recently left their agency. At the first attack, all were struck, Private Smith mortally, and three others severely wounded. Although enclosed on all sides, and by overwhelming numbers, one of them succeeded, while they were under severe fire at short range, and while the others with their rifles were keeping the Indians at bay, in digging, with his knife and hands, a slight cover. After this had been secured, they placed themselves within it, the wounded walking with brave and painful effort, and Private Smith — though he had received a mortal wound — sitting upright within the trench, to conceal the crippled condition of the party from the Indians.

"From early morning until dark, outnumbered twenty-five to one, under an almost constant fire, and at such short range that they sometimes used their pistols, retaining the last charge to prevent capture and torture, this little party of five men defended their lives and the person of their dying comrade, without food, and their only drink the rainwater that collected in a pool mingled with their own blood. There was no doubt that they killed more than double their own number, besides those that were wounded. The Indians abandoned the attack on the 12th at dark.

"The exposure and distance from the command, which were necessary incidents of their duty, were such that for twenty-six hours from the first attack, their condition could not be known, and not until midnight of the 13th could they receive medical attention and food, exposed during this time to an incessant cold storm.

"Sergt. Woodall, Private Harrington and Scout Chapman were seriously wounded. Private Smith died of his wounds on the morning of the 13th. Private Rath and Scout Dixon were struck, but not disabled.

"The simple recital of their deeds, and the mention of odds against which they fought — how the wounded defended the dying, and the dying aided the wounded by exposure to fresh wounds, after the power of action had gone — these alone present a scene of cool courage, heroism and self-sacrifice which duty, as well as inclination, prompts us to recognize, but which we cannot fitly honor.

"Very resp'y your obedient servant,

"NELSON A. MILES,
"Colonel and Bvt. Maj. Gen.
"U. S. A. Commanding."

Two stories have been told in print of this desperate defense — one by Billy Dixon, one of the most courageous, cool and renowned army scouts of the '70's, who died in 1913 — and one by Amos Chapman, also a well-known army scout and Indian fighter. Chapman died in 1925 at Seiling, Oklahoma.

For fifty years Chapman posed as the real hero of the noted "buffalo wallow" Indian battle. Billy Dixon, on the other hand, with his well-known modesty, refrained from disputing the claim of Chapman.

The author believes in fair play and in giving honor where honor is due. Therefore, the stories of both Dixon and Chapman are here given, together with an affidavit from Sergt. Woodall, written in 1889. The reader must then form his own conclusions as to which of the two men is entitled to the distinction of being the real hero of the buffalo wallow fight. Dixon's story was supplied the

BILLY DIXON, FAMOUS SCOUT AND FRONTIERSMAN IN 1874. THIS
PHOTO TAKEN JUST BEFORE HIS DEATH IN 1912. PHOTO
COURTESY MRS. OLIVE K. DIXON, MIAMI, TEXAS.

author by Mrs. Olive Dixon, wife of the noted scout, today a well-known and brilliant newspaper woman of Miami, Texas, and is as follows:

"The most perilous adventure of my life occurred September 12, 1874, in what was known as the 'Buffalo Wallow fight.' My escape from death was miraculous. During that year I came in contact with hostile Indians as frequently as the most devoted warrior might wish, and found that it was a serious business.

"On September 10, 1874, Gen. Nelson A. Miles, in command of the troops campaigning against the Indians in the Southwest, was on McClellan Creek, in the Texas Panhandle, when he ordered Amos Chapman and myself, (scouts) and four enlisted men, to carry dispatches to Camp Supply. The enlisted men were Sergt. Z. T. Woodall, Troop I; Private Peter Rath, Troop A; Private John Harrington, Troop H, and Private George W. Smith, Troop M, Sixth Cavalry. When General Miles handed us the dispathes he told us we could have all the soldiers we thought necessary for an escort. His command was short of rations. We preferred the smallest possible number.

"Leaving camp we traveled mostly at night, resting in secluded places during the day. War parties were moving in every direction, and there was danger of attack at every turn.

"On the second day, just as the sun was rising, we were nearing a divide between the Washita River and Gageby Creek. Riding to the top of a little knoll, we found ourselves face to face with a large band of Kiowa and Comanche Indians. The Indians saw us at the same time, and circling quickly, surrounded us. We were in a trap. We knew that the best thing to do was to make a stand and fight for our lives, as there would be great danger of our becoming separated in the excitement of a running fight, after which the Indians could then more easily kill us one by one. We also realized that we could do better work on foot; so we dismounted and placed our horses in the care of George Smith. In a moment or two poor Smith was shot down, and the horses stampeded.

"When Smith was shot he fell flat on his stomach, and his gun fell from his hands, far from reach. But no Indian was able to capture that gun. If one ventured near Smith we never failed to bring him down. We thought Smith was dead when he fell; but he survived until about 11 o'clock that night.

"I realized at once that I was in closer quarters than I had ever been in my life, and I have always felt that I did some good work that day. I was fortunate enough not to become disabled at any stage of the fight, which left me free to do my best under the circumstances. I received one wound — a bullet in the calf of the leg. I was wearing a thin cashmere shirt, slightly bloused. This shirt was literally riddled with bullets. How a man could be shot at so many times at close range and not be hit, I never could understand. The Indians seemed absolutely sure of getting us — so sure, in fact, that they delayed riding us down and killing us at once — which they could easily have done, and prolonged the early stages of the fight merely to satisfy their desire to toy with an enemy, as a cat would play with a mouse before taking its life.

"We saw that there was no show for us to survive on this little hillside, and decided that our best fighting ground was a small mesquite flat, several hundred yards distant. Before we undertook to shift our position, a bullet struck Amos Chapman. I was looking at him when he was shot. Amos said, 'Billy, I am hit at last,' and eased himself down. The fight was so hot that I did not have time to ask him how badly he was hurt. Every man, save Rath and myself, had been wounded. Our situation was growing more desperate every minute. I knew that something had to be done, and quickly, or else all of us, in a short time, would be dead or in the hands of the Indians, who would torture us in the most inhuman manner before taking our lives.

"I could see where herds of buffalo had pawed and wallowed a depression commonly called a 'buffalo wallow,' and I ran for it at top speed. It seemed as if a bullet whizzed past me at every jump, but I got through unharmed. The wallow was about ten feet in diameter. I found that its depth, though slight, afforded some protection. I shouted to my comrades to try and come to me, which all of them, save Smith and Chapman, commenced trying to do. As each man reached the wallow, he drew his butcher knife and began digging desperately, with knife and hands, to throw up dirt around the sides. The land happened to be sandy, and we made good headway, though constantly interrupted by the necessity of firing at the Indians as they dashed within range.

"Many times during that terrible day did I think that my last moment was at hand. Once, when the Indians were crowding us awfully hard, one of the boys raised up and yelled, 'No use, boys; no use; we might as well give up!' We answered by shouting to him to lie down. At that moment a bullet struck in the soft bank near him, filling his mouth with dirt. I was so amused that I laughed, though in a sickly way, for none of us felt like laughing.

"By this time, however, I had recovered from the first excitement of battle, and was perfectly cool, as were the rest of the men. We were keenly aware that the only thing to do was to sell our lives as dearly as possible. We fired deliberately, taking good aim, and were picking off an Indian at almost every round. The wounded men conducted themselves admirably, and greatly assisted in concealing our crippled condition by sitting upright, as if unhurt, after they reached the wallow. This made it impossible for the Indians to accurately guess what plight we were in. Had they known so many of us were wounded, undoubtedly they would have ridden in and finished us.

"After all had reached the wallow, with the exception of Chapman and Smith, all of us thinking that Smith was dead, somebody called to Chapman to come on in. We now learned for the first time that Chapman's leg was broken. He called back that he could not walk, as his left knee was shattered.

"I made several efforts to reach him before I succeeded. Every time the Indians saw me start, they would fire such a volley that I was forced to retreat; until finally I made a run and got to Chapman. I

BILLY DIXON, SCOUT AND GUIDE FOR THE U. S. GOVERNMENT
NINE YEARS. PHOTO TAKEN ABOUT 1880. PHOTO COURTESY
MRS. OLIVE K. DIXON, MIAMI, TEXAS.

told him to climb on my back, my plan being to carry him as I would a little child. Drawing both his legs in front of me and laying the broken one over the sound one, to support it, I carried him to the wallow, though not without great difficulty, as he was a larger man than myself, and his body a dead weight. It taxed my strength to carry him.

"We were now all in the wallow except Smith, and we felt that it would be foolish and useless to risk our lives in attempting to bring in his supposedly dead body. We had not seen him move since the moment he went down. We began digging like gophers with our hands and knives to make our little wall of earth higher, and shortly had heaped up quite a little wall of dirt around us. Its protection was quickly felt, even though our danger was hardly lessened.

"When I look back and recall our situation I always find myself wondering and thinking of the manner in which my wounded comrades acted — never complaining or faltering, but they fought as bravely as if a bullet had not touched them. Sometimes the Indians would ride toward us at headlong speed, with lances uplifted and poised, undoubtedly bent upon spearing us. Such moments made a man brace himself and grip his gun. Fortunately, we were able to keep our heads, and to bring down or disable the leader. Such charges proved highly dangerous to the Indians, and gradually grew less frequent.

"Thus, all that long September day, the Indians circled around us or dashed past, yelling and cutting up all kinds of capers. All morning we had been without water, and the wounded were sorely in need of it. In the stress and excitement of such an encounter, even a man who has not been hurt, grows painfully thirsty, and his tongue and lips are soon as dry as a whetstone. Ours was the courage of despair. We knew what would befall us if captured alive — we had seen too many naked and mangled bodies of white men who had been spread eagled and tortured with steel and fire, to forget what our own fate would be. So we were determined to fight to the end, not mindful of the fact that every once in a while there was another dead or wounded Indian.

"About three o'clock a black cloud came up in the west, and in a short time the sky shook and blazed with thunder and lightning. Rain fell in blinding sheets, drenching us to the skin. Water gathered quickly in the buffalo wallow, and our wounded men eagerly bent forward and drank from the muddy pool. It was more than muddy — that water was red with their own blood that had flowed from their wounds, and lay clotting and dry in the hot September sun.

"The storm and rain proved our salvation. The wind had shifted to the north, and was now drearily chilling us to the bone. An Indian dislikes rain, especially a cold rain, and those Kiowas and Comanches were no exception to the rule. We could see them in groups out of rifle range, sitting on their ponies with their blankets drawn tightly around them. The plains country beats the world for quick changes in weather, and in less than an hour after the rain had fallen, the wind was bitter cold. Not a man in our crowd had a coat, and our thin shirts were scant protection. Our coats were tied behind our saddles when our horses stampeded, and were lost beyond recovery. I was heartsick over the loss of my coat, for in the inside pocket was my dearest treasure — my mother's picture, which my father had given me shortly before his death. I was never able to recover it.

"The water was gathering rapidly in the wallow, and soon reached a depth of two inches, but not a man murmured. Not one thought of surrender, although the wounded were shivering as if they had the ague.

"We now found that our ammunition was running low. This fact rather appalled us, as bullets — and plenty of them — were our only protection. Necessity compelled us to husband every cartridge as long as possible, and not to fire at an Indian unless we could see that he meant business, and was coming right into us.

"Late in the afternoon somebody suggested that we should go out and get Smith's belt and six-shooter, as he had been shot early in the fight, and his belt was undoubtedly loaded with cartridges.

"Rath offered to go, and soon returned with the startling information that Smith was still alive! This astonished us greatly, and caused us deep regret that we had not known it earlier in the day. Rath and I at once got ready to bring poor Smith to the buffalo wallow. By supporting the wounded man between us, he managed to walk. We could see that there was no chance for him. He was shot through the left lung, and when he breathed the wind sobbed out of his back under the left shoulder blade. Near the wallow an Indian had dropped a stout willow switch with which he had been whipping his pony. Using this switch a silk handkerchief was forced into the gaping hole in Smith's back to staunch the flow of blood, in a measure.

"Night was approaching, and it looked blacker to me than any night I had ever seen. Ours was a forlorn and disheartening situation. The Indians were still all around us. The nearest relief was seventy-five miles away. Of the six men in the wallow, four were badly wounded, and without anything to relieve their suffering. We were cold and hungry, with nothing to eat, and without a blanket, coat or hat to protect us from the rain and the biting wind. It was impossible to rest or sleep with two inches of water in the wallow.

"I remember that I threw my hat — a wide-brimmed sombrero — as far from me as I could when our horses stampeded. The hat was in my way, and further, was too good a target for the Indians to shoot at.

"We were unable to get grass for bedding for the reason that the whole country had been burned over by the Indians. It was absolutely necessary, however, that the men should have some kind of bed to keep them off the cold, damp ground. Rath and I solved the problem by gathering tumble-weeds, which in that country the wind would drive for miles and miles. Many of them were bigger than a bushel basket, and their sprigs so tough that the weeds had the 'spring' of a wire mattress. We crushed the weeds down and lay down on them for the night, though not a man dared close his eyes in sleep.

"By the time heavy darkness had fallen, every Indian had disappeared. Happily, they did not return to molest us during the night, although, of course, we had nothing to assure us that we would not be again attacked. There was a new moon, but so small and slender that in the clouded sky there was but little light. While there was yet a little daylight left I took the willow switch, and sitting down on the edge of our improvised little fort, I carefully cleaned every gun.

"While engaged in this occupation we held a council to decide what was the best thing to do. We agreed that somebody must go for help. No journey could have been beset with greater danger. Rath and I both offered to go. In fact, the task was squarely up to us, as all the other men were too badly injured. I insisted that I should go, as I knew the country, and felt confident that I could find the trail that led to Camp Supply. I was sure we were not far from the trail.

"My insistence at once caused protest from the wounded. They were willing that Rath should go, but would not listen to my leaving them. Once I put my hand on my gun, with the intention of going anyway, then I yielded to their wishes against my better judgment, and decided to remain through the night. The wounded men relied greatly on my skill as a marksman.

"Rath, therefore, made ready for the journey, and then bidding us goodby he crawled away into the darkness. In about two hours, while we were hoping he had managed to get a good start without being detected, he returned, saying he could not locate the trail.

"By this time Smith had grown much worse, and was begging us, in piteous tones, to shoot him and put an end to his terrible agony. We found it necessary to watch him closely to prevent his committing suicide.

"There was not a man among us who had not thought of the same melancholy fate. When the fighting was at its worst, with the Indians closing in on all sides, and when it seemed that every minute would be our last, it was only by our great coolness and marksmanship that we kept the savages from getting in among us, which would probably have compelled us to use the last shot on ourselves. At that time I was wearing my hair long and as I had quite a crop of it, I knew it would be a great temptation to the Indians to get my scalp.

"Poor Smith endured his agony like a brave soldier. Our hearts ached for him, and we longed to relieve his suffering, but there was absolutely nothing that we could do for him. About 1 o'clock that night he fell asleep, and we were glad of it, for in sleep he could forget his sufferings. Later in the night one of the boys felt of him to see how he was getting along. Poor Smith! He was cold in death. Men commonly think of death as something to be shunned, but there are times when its hand falls as tenderly as the touch of a mother's, and when its coming is welcomed by those to whom hopeless suffering had brought the last bitter dregs of life. We lifted the body of our dead comrade and gently laid

GEN. NELSON A. MILES.

(122)

it outside the buffalo wallow on the mesquite grass, covering the face with a white silk handkerchief.

"That was a night to try men's souls! What fate would the morrow have in store for us? It was a night that is indelibly stamped on my memory, and which time can never efface. Many a time since has its perils filled my dreams, until I awoke, startled and thrilled, with a feeling of most imminent danger. Every night the same stars are shining way out there in the lonely Panhandle country; the same winds sigh as mournfully as they did on that terrible night, and I often wonder if a single settler, who passes the lonely spot, knows how desperately six men once battled for their lives, where now, perhaps, plowed fields and safety, with all the comforts of civilization, are on every hand.

"Like everything else the long, dreary night at length came to an end, and the first rosy tints of dawn tinged the eastern sky, while the sun came out clear and warm. By this time all the men were willing that I should go for help. Our perilous position was such that there must be no waiting for darkness to cover my movements; it was imperative that I start immediately, and bidding them all be of good cheer I started. Daylight exposed me to many dangers from which the night shielded me. By moving cautiously at night, it was possible to avoid an enemy, and even if surprised there was a chance to escape in the darkness. But in the broad daylight the enemy could lie in hiding and sweep the country with keen eyes in every direction. On the plains — especially in the fall — when the grass was short and there was no cover, the smallest moving object could be perceived by such trained eyes as hostile Indians possessed, at an astonishing long distance. I knew I must proceed with the utmost caution, lest I fall into an ambush or be attacked in the open by superior numbers.

"I had traveled scarcely more than half a mile from the wallow when I struck the plain trail leading to Camp Supply. Hurrying along as rapidly as possible, and keeping a constant lookout for Indians, I suddenly checked myself at the sight of moving objects about two miles to the northwest, which seemed to cover about an acre of ground. At first the objects did not appear to be moving, and I could not tell whether it was Indians or white men. I skulked to a growth of tall grass and lay in hiding for a brief time. My nerves, however, were too keen to endure this, so I cautiously raised myself and took another look. The outfit was moving toward me. Shortly, I was enabled to discern that it was a body of troops. Indians always traveled strung out in a line, but these were traveling abreast.

"I never felt happier in all my life! I stepped out into the open and whanged away with my rifle to attract their attention. The whole command suddenly came to a halt. I fired a second shot, and presently saw two men ride out from the command toward me. When they came up, I told them my story and reported the serious condition of my comrades. The soldiers rode rapidly back to the command and reported. It proved to be a detachment under the command of Major Price, accompanying General Miles' supply train, which was on its way from Camp Supply to field headquarters.

"It appeared that the same Indians we had been fighting had been holding this supply train corraled for four days near the Washita river. Major Price happened along and raised the siege. The Indians had just given up the attack on this train when we happened to run into them.

"Major Price rode out where I was waiting, bringing his army surgeon with him. I described the condition of my comrades, after which the major instructed his surgeon and two soldiers to go and see what could be done for my wounded comrades. I pointed out the location, which was not more than a mile distant, and asked the surgeon if he thought he could find the place without my accompanying him, as Major Price wanted me to remain and tell him about the fight. He said he could, and they rode away.

"I was describing in detail all that had happened, when I looked up and noted that the relief party was bearing too far toward the south. I fired my gun to attract their attention, and then waved it in the direction I intended they should go. By this time they were within gunshot of the wallow. Suddenly, to my utter astonishment, I saw a puff of smoke rise from the wallow, followed by the roar of a rifle — one of the men had fired at the approaching strangers, and dropped a horse ridden by one of the soldiers.

"I ran forward as rapidly as possible, not knowing what the men might do next. They were soon able to recognize me, and lowered their guns. When we got to them the men said they heard shooting — the shots I had fired to attract the attention of the troops—and supposed the Indians had killed me and were coming back to renew the attack upon them. They were determined to take no chances, and not recognizing the surgeon and the two soldiers, had fired at them the minute they got within range.

"Despite the sad plight of the wounded men, about all the surgeon did was merely examine their wounds. The soldiers turned over a few bits of hardtack and some dried beef which happened to be tied behind their saddles. Major Price further refused to leave any men with us. For this he was afterward severely censured — and justly. He would not even provide us with firearms. Our own ammunition was exhausted, and the soldiers carried weapons of a different make and caliber than our own. However, they said they would let General Miles know of our condition. We were sure that help would come the instant the general heard the news.

"We watched and waited until midnight of the second day after these troops had passed, before help came. A long way off in the darkness we heard the sound of a bugle. Never was there sweeter music than that to our suffering nerves! It made us swallow a big lump in our throats. Nearer and nearer came the bugle notes. We fired our guns with the few remaining cartridges we had, and soon the soldiers came riding to us out of the darkness.

"As soon as the wounded could be turned over to the surgeon, we placed the dead body of our comrade in the wallow where we had fought and suffered together, and covered it with the dirt which we had ridged up with our hands and butcher knives.

Then we went down on the creek, where the soldiers had built a big fire, and cooked a big meal for us.

"Next day the wounded were sent to Camp Supply. Amos Chapman's leg was amputated above the knee. All the men eventually recovered, and went right on with the army. Chapman could handle a gun and ride as well as ever, but had to mount his horse from the right side, Indian fashion.

"When I last heard from Amos Chapman he was living at Seiling, Oklahoma. In the early '80's, Col. Richard Irving Dodge, U. S. A., wrote a book entitled 'Our Wild Indians,' in which he attempted to give a circumstantial account of the buffalo wallow fight. Sergt. Woodall was displeased with the statement of facts therein, and resented the inaccuracies.

"When Colonel Dodge was writing his book, he wrote to me and asked me to send him an account of the buffalo wallow fight. I neglected to do so, and he obtained his information from other sources. If my narrative differs from that related in Colonel Dodge's book, all I can say is that I have described the fight as I saw it. In saying this, I do not wish to place myself in the attitude of censuring Colonel Dodge. However, it should be reasonably apparent that a man with a broken leg cannot carry another man on his back. In correcting this bit of border warfare history I wish to state that every one of my comrades conducted himself in the most heroic manner, bravely doing his part in every emergency.

"General Miles had both the heart and the accomplishments of a soldier, and Congress voted to each of us the Medal of Honor. He was delighted when the medals came from Washington, and with his own hands pinned mine on my coat when we were in camp on Carson Creek, five or six miles west of the ruins of the original Adobe Walls.

"It was always my intention to return and mark the spot where the buffalo wallow fight took place, and where George Smith yet lies buried. Procrastination and the remoteness of the place have prevented this."

———

Now for the story which appears on page 631 of Colonel Dodge's well-known book, "Our Wild Indians," which was brought out in 1882:

"Heroic as was the conduct of all, that of Chapman deserves most special honor, for he received his wound while performing a deed than which the loftiest manhood can find nothing nobler.

"The first intimation of the presence of the Indians was a volley which wounded every man in the party. In an instant the Indians appeared on all sides! Dismounting and abandoning their horses, the brave band moved together for a hundred yards to a buffalo wallow. Chapman and Dixon being but slightly wounded, worked hard and fast to deepen this depression, and as soon as it was satisfactorily deep to afford some cover, it was occupied. Smith had fallen from his horse at the first fire, and was supposed to be dead. Now the supposed dead body was seen to move slightly. He was alive, though entirely disabled. Turning to his comrades, Chapman said: 'Now, boys, keep those infernal redskins off of me, and I will run down and pick up Smith and bring him back before they can get at me.'

"Laying down his rifle, he sprang out of the buffalo wallow and ran with all speed to Smith and attempted to shoulder him. 'Did any of you ever try to shoulder a wounded man?' asked Chapman, in relating the story. 'Smith was not a large man —160 or 170 pounds — but I declare to you that he seemed to weigh a ton. Finally I laid him down and got his chest across my back and his arms around my neck, and then got up with him. It was as much as I could do to stagger under him, for he couldn't help himself a bit. By the time I had got twenty or thirty yards, about fifteen Indians came at me at full speed on their ponies. They all knew me and yelled, 'Amos, Amos, we have got you now!' I pulled my pistol, but I couldn't hold Smith on my back with one hand, so I let him drop. The boys in the buffalo wallow opened on the Indians just at the right time, and I opened on them with my pistol. There was a tumbling of ponies and a scattering of Indians, and in a minute they were gone. I got Smith up again and made the best possible time, but before I could reach the wallow another gang came for me. I had only one or two shots in my pistol, so I didn't stop to fight, but ran for it. When I was within twenty yards of the wallow, a little old scoundrel that I had fed fifty times, rode almost on me and fired. I fell, with Smith on top of me, *but as I didn't feel any pain*, I thought I had stepped into a hole. I jumped up, picked up Smith and got safe in the wallow. 'Amos,' said Dixon, 'you are badly hurt.' 'No, I am not,' said I. 'Why look at your leg,' and sure enough, the leg was shot off just above the ankle joint, *and I had been walking on the bone, dragging the foot behind me; and in the excitement I never knew it, nor have I ever had any pain in my leg to this day."*

———————

The author had read this account of the buffalo wallow fight, as related by Amos Chapman in Col. Richard I. Dodge's "Our Wild Indians," probably a hundred times as a small boy — in fact, it was one of his pet stories, and he always marveled at the cool courage of a man who could pack a 170-pound comrade on his back with his own leg shot off at the ankle joint!

It was not until about 1920, however, that Billy Dixon's account of this battle was discovered and read by the author. There was such a vast difference between the two stories that the author immediately became interested, and wondered if Amos Chapman was stealing Billy Dixon's thunder, or vice versa. A little quiet investigation followed. Amos Chapman was at that time living in Seiling, Oklahoma. The author wrote him, calling his attention to the great difference between the Chapman story and the Dixon account of the battle, and asking if he know which was correct. No reply was ever received. Not knowing but what Chapman might be dead, the author then wrote to an attorney of Seiling, and received a reply that he (the attorney) could tell anything about Amos Chapman which the author might wish to know. His attention was, therefore, called to the two stories, and he was asked if he would query Chapman about it. Nothing further was ever heard from the attorney, although he was again addressed once or twice.

The author then opened communication with Mrs. Olive K. Dixon, at Miami, Texas, widow of Billy Dixon. She was at first loth to say anything on the subject, but finally, after being questioned, and reminded that, for the sake of history, and for the reputation of her dead husband, the actual facts should be made public, she sent the author the following letter, written under date of January 4, 1880, by Sergt. Z. T. Woodall, first sergeant, Troop I, 6th U. S. Cavalry, one of the four soldiers in the fight, from Fort Wingate, N. M., where he was then stationed. It would seem that this letter disproves entirely the Chapman story and proves very conclusively that Billy Dixon, the intrepid scout, was the real hero in the buffalo wallow engagement.

"Fort Wingate, N. M.,
Jan. 4, 1889.

"FRIEND DIXON:

"Hearing that you were at Adobe Walls in the Panhandle of Texas, and as we both came near passing in our checks between the Gageby Creek and the Washita river on September 12, 1874, I thought it would not be out of place to drop you a few lines and revive old times. I heard from a man by the name of Shearer who belonged to the Fourth Cavalry, that you were there.

"Do you ever see Amos, or any of the men who were with us then? I never have, and would very much like to see any of them and fight our old fights over again.

"Did you read the account (in *Our Wild Indians*) where Amos carried Smith on his back, and did not know his leg was shot off until he got to the wallow? *Did you ever hear tell of such a damn lie, when he knows very well that you carried both of them there yourself?* I was surprised when I read the account in the book written by Col. Dodge. To read it you would think that there was no one there but Chapman himself. The idea that a man could have his leg shot off and did not know it, makes me tired. You can bet that I came very near knowing it when I was struck, and I know it and feel it to this day, and my leg was not shot off. When I read the book I came very near contradicting it, as there were others who did just as much as Chapman, if not more. It seems that when he met Col. Dodge he took all the credit to himself * * * Dixon, don't fail to answer this letter, because I would sooner hear from you than any man that I know of, and give me your opinion of the fight. I would have written you before, but did not know where you were. I will close this letter with my best wishes for your welfare.

"From your sincere friend, and one on whom you can depend under any and all circumstances.

(Signed) "Z. T. WOODALL,

"1st Sergeant, Troop I, 6th Cavalry,

"Fort Wingate, N. M."

STATE OF TEXAS,

COUNTY OF ROBERTS.

I hereby certify that I have compared the above letter (copy of a certified copy of a letter) written by Z. T. Woodall, now in possession of Mrs. Olive

Dixon, of Miami, Texas, and the above copy is true and correct to the best of my knowledge and belief.

H. A. TULLEY.

Subscribed and sworn to before me as a notary public in and for Roberts county, Texas, this the 27th day of Jan. A. D. 1923.

JAS. Z. SAUL, Notary Public.

My commission expires June 1, 1923.

————

With no other desire save to give "honor to whom honor is due," and wishing to make public only *true* frontier history, the author determined that it was high time — after a lapse of fifty years — that the public should know *who* was the real hero in the buffalo wallow engagement, and that the hosts of Billy Dixon's friends throughout the country, who remember him with only words of praise and commendation, should be given the true facts of the case, and his name placed on the pinnacle of fame where it rightfully belongs.

To that end, the facts were published in the HUNTER-TRADER-TRAPPER, in March, 1925, and the suggestion was made by the author that a monument or marker should be placed on the site of this noted Indian fight. Mrs. Dixon, meantime, was soliciting funds and creating interest in the matter, and in due time sufficient money had been raised to purchase a suitable monument, properly lettered, which will shortly be installed on the site of the buffalo wallow battle, which is in Hemphill county, Texas, twenty-two miles south of the town of Canadian, and twenty-five miles southeast of Miami, on land owned by W. M. Wright, of Gageby, Texas.

The site was definitely located in April, 1921, by J. J. Long, of Mobeetie, Texas, who at the time of the battle, was a teamster in the wagon-train hauling supplies for Gen. Miles' army. Billy Dixon and Mr. Long became close friends, and a short time after, when Long was a mail carrier between Fort Elliott, Texas, and Camp Supply, Indian Territory, and Billy Dixon was serving as a guard, or escort, for the mail, their route took them over the ground on which the fight occurred, and Dixon and Long would frequently halt at the site, while the former would relate incidents of the battle as they were recalled. Mr. Long was, therefore, very familiar with the lay of the land, and in 1921 had no trouble in locating the exact spot of this thrilling Indian engagement.

BUFFALO WALLOW MEMORIAL, MADE POSSIBLE THROUGH THE HELP OF H-T-T READERS.

CHAPTER V

TOBEY RIDDLE — MODOC INDIAN WAR HEROINE

THE STORY OF A BRAVE INDIAN WOMAN'S DEVOTION TO DUTY.

DURING the latter part of February, 1920, there died on the Klamath Indian Reservation in Southern Oregon, a Modoc Indian woman, full of years and honor. Her maiden name was "Wi-ne-ma," but she was better known among her own people and the whites simply as "Tobey" Riddle. When but a young girl she was wooed and won by a white man named Frank Riddle, an honest, kind, temperate and thoughtful miner. She quickly learned to speak the white man's tongue, and in time both she and her "man" became expert interpreters, rendering valuable service when the Indian Department held "pow-wows" with the Modoc tribe. Frank Riddle died in 1906, honored and respected by all who knew him.

It was during the Modoc war of 1873 that Tobey Riddle performed her greatest service to the United States government, which resulted, some years later, in her being granted a pension of $25 a month for the balance of her life. The Modocs had taken to the warpath — or rather had been driven to it through the avarice, greed and unscrupulous dealings of the white man — (which has been the initial cause of every Indian war in America). After the first hot preliminary skirmish with the United States troops which had been sent against them, together with some Oregon volunteers, fifty-two Modoc warriors, under their chief, known as "Captain Jack," (who was a full cousin to Tobey Riddle) representing the total fighting force of the tribe, with upwards of 150 women, old men and children, retreated to the "Lava Beds," a barren, inaccessible, volcanic section of country just across the northern line of California, and for several weeks defied and held at bay more than one thousand United States troops, with appalling results to the soldiers, and with but infinitesimal loss to the Indians.

After several attempts to induce the Indians to surrender, during which time several "peace talks" were indulged in, a meeting was arranged for the 11th of April, 1873, to be held midway between the camp of the troops and the stronghold of the Modocs. Both sides agreed to come to the council unarmed. Each was represented by six persons. The Commissioners went to the meeting unarmed, except two men, who carried small Deringer pistols. The Indians, under the leadership of Captain Jack, were all armed with revolvers hidden beneath their blankets. While the council was in progress, the Indians suddenly threw aside their blankets, grasped their hidden weapons and opened fire upon the defenseless Commissioners. Two were killed outright, two saved themselves by their fleetness of foot, and one was shot down and a Modoc brave was already scalping him, when Tobey Riddle flung herself upon the savage, fighting him with superhuman strength; then shouting that "soldiers are coming!" The Modocs thereupon fled back to their stronghold. The wounded commissioner was revived, and after several weeks of careful nursing at the hands of Tobey Riddle, recovered.

The Modoc war was the most costly to the United States of any in which it ever engaged, considering the number of opponents. And the Modocs were not subdued until after a difficulty had arisen in their own ranks, which resulted in a division of their forces, one faction finally surrendering to the soldiers, then turning about, playing traitor and assisting in trailing down their red brothers, who were finally captured. Four of the ringleaders, including Captain Jack, were hanged, and two others were imprisoned for life. During the fighting the Modocs lost but twelve warriors killed, while the total loss of white settlers and soldiers numbered 168. The cost of the war to the United States government was in excess of $500,000.

The first trouble with the Modocs started in 1853, when some Pitt River Indians waylaid and killed some settlers who were enroute to California. A few made their escape and reached Yreka, California, where they gave the alarm. Here a company of sixty-five fighting men was raised to go out and punish the hostile Pitt River savages who had attacked the emigrants. The guilty tribe was not overtaken, but the miners, in their search, came upon some of the Hot Creek Modocs. The Modocs had always lived at peace with the whites, but to the enraged miners "an Injun was an Injun," and

CAPTAIN JACK, MODOC CHIEF.

(138)

they opened fire upon the inoffensive Modocs. Only a few escaped, while several women and children were victims of the miners' fury.

The flame had now been fanned, and for some years trouble was rife. Capt. Jack's father was at that time chief of the tribe, and he counseled war against the white invaders, but the son stood firmly for peace. In 1856 occurred another disastrous affair, in which one Ben Wright, heading a company of volunteers, invited a band of nearly half a hundred Modocs to come to a feast which he had prepared for them. The Modocs were assured that the volunteers were their friends. Wright told them he was a "peacemaker." The Indians believed him. The Modocs moved their camp in close to that of the soldiers. The next morning, before daybreak, the soldiers surrounded the tepees of the unsuspecting Modocs and opened fire on them. Only five escaped.

Three years later white settlers began coming into the country occupied by the Modocs. Captain Jack was now chief of the tribe, his father having fallen a victim to the treachery of Ben Wright's volunteers. Jack welcomed the white settlers, and there was no more trouble between them and the Modocs for some time. Finally a difficulty arose between a white man named Ball and one of the Modocs, and the two men became bitter enemies. Ball complained to Captain Knapp, agent at Klamath Reservation, that the Modocs were stealing cattle from the whites, as well as demanding provisions. He stated further that he "feared the Modocs were preparing for war" — when nothing of the sort was premeditated, nor were the Modocs stealing cattle and provisions, as had been alleged.

However, the government (always quick to side against the Indians) appointed Col. A. B. Meacham as a Peace Commissioner to visit Captain Jack and determine the cause of the reported trouble. After a conference, at which Frank Riddle and his Indian wife, Tobey, acted as interpreters, the Modocs were told that the government had decided to send them to the Klamath agency to make that spot their future home.

Captain Jack raised no objections to this removal. It was effected without the least trouble. But the Klamaths did not take kindly to this new state of affairs, and immediately began quarreling with their new neighbors, telling them they had no business to come there and infringe upon their territory, and stating that they (the Klamaths) owned that part of the country. They further advised the Modocs to go back to Tule Lake, their old home. Captain Jack sought the agent and asked protection from the offending Klamaths. The agent haughtily informed the chief that he "wouldn't be bothered with his complaints." The following day Captain Jack and his entire following quietly packed up and went back on the banks of Lost River to their old camping ground, where the white settlers told them "there is plenty of room for us all."

Thus matters continued harmoniously until September, 1872. Ball, the troublesome white settler, had left while the Modocs were on the Klamath Reservation. Then word was received that soldiers were coming to compel the Modocs to move back to the Klamath Reservation. Tobey Riddle rode seventy-five miles on horseback to warn her people that the troops were to be sent after them. The Modocs thereupon told the settlers about them, that they expected trouble with the troops when they arrived, and advised them to take no action themselves against the Modocs, nor affiliate with the soldiers if fighting broke out. "Let the soldiers whip us if they can," advised the Modocs. They then returned to their lodges, satisfied that an understanding with their white neighbors had been effected.

The following morning, true to the report, the Modocs awoke in their tepees to find their camp surrounded by troops under Major Jackson. The latter demanded to see Captain Jack. The chief appeared and was informed that the "Great Father" at Washington had sent the soldiers there to get him and all his people and compel them to go back to the Klamath Reservation again. Captain Jack quietly informed Major Jackson that he and his people would obey the mandate of the Great Father. The chief was then informed that before the Modocs started for the reservation, they must surrender their arms. A heated discussion followed, but Captain Jack quieted his braves and ordered them to lay down their guns. All obeyed but one Indian, who insisted upon retaining an old pistol. Lieut. Boutelle drew his own revolver and ordered this warrior to deposit his pistol with the other surrendered arms. As Boutelle leveled his revolver, the Indian snatched out his own weapon. Both fired at the same instant. Immediately the soldiers opened a general fire upon the unarmed Modocs, who rushed for their weapons, secured many of them and returned the fire of the troops. Two dead and several wounded on each side was the result of this little skirmish.

The settlers now rushed to the assistance of the troops and a general fight ensued. The Modocs retreated to the Lava Beds. Here preparations for a most determined resistance were begun. Jack's forces were increased to fifty-two fighting men, but he was also burdened with about 150 women, old men and little children. The Lava Beds comprised a section of territory about eight miles long and four wide. They formed a perfect network of obstructions, and with their volcanic formation resembled great ocean waves "frozen solid" in great billows. Transversal crevices furnished most excellent communication whereby the Indians were enabled to pass from one ridge to another without exposing themselves in the least. Every inch of this territory was known to the Modocs. Various caves were discovered in the series of ridges which could be easily blockaded by rolling heavy stones before the entrances. It was a spot in which a handful of men could defy a hundred times their number as long as they had food and ammunition.

In this natural fortification the Modocs rested and took life easy after their initial battle with Major Jackson's men. They kept sentinels on guard day and night, and every movement of the troops was known to them. On January 15, 1873, horsemen were seen approaching, and they were soon identified as soldiers. They were under the command of General Gillem. Gillem looked the situation over and then made preparations to advance on the Modoc stronghold on the 17th. He was instructed to "rout the Modocs." The soldiers were inclined to look upon the whole proceeding as a huge joke. The idea that half a hundred Indians would put up a fight against two or three hundred seasoned troops was well calculated to start much jesting, and many of the soldiers discussed with great gusto the "Modoc steaks" they intended to have for dinner. It was even inferred that "there won't be half enough Modocs to go around."

The morning of the 17th dawned clear and cloudless. The troops were impatient to start the drive. Not an Indian was to be seen, as the troops advanced toward the Lava Beds. It was hinted that "them Injuns have hot-footed as sure as shootin'." The officers were impatient. "We'll show you dead Indians if you'll show us live ones," they assured their scouts.

Suddenly a single shot rang out from the Modoc stronghold. An officer pitched forward to the ground, dead. This was followed by other shots from the concealed redskins, although the troopers were unable to see an Indian; but the continual crack of rifles caused great confusion among the troops. Volley after volley was poured in the direction of the Modocs. The latter knew every crack and fissure of their fortifications, and they never exposed themselves an inch. There were abundant crevices through which they could fire, and their deadly accuracy caused a panic among the soldiers. Finally, a heavy fog blew in from Tule Lake, and this made the advance of the soldiers more precarious than

TOBEY RIDDLE, HEROINE OF THE MODOC WAR, FROM A PHOTO
TAKEN IN 1873. COPYRIGHTED BY MAJOR GEO. INGALLS.

ever. Men fell dead and wounded every time an
advance was ordered. Thus matters continued all
day, when the soldiers withdrew to their camp with
their dead and wounded. It had been a most unlucky day for them. "During the whole day,"
records one officer who took part in the fighting,
"I did not see an Indian, nor do I recall that anyone else did. The Modocs simply held us there until
darkness permitted us to retreat."

When Captain Jack called his roll that night there
was not even a wounded Indian among his forces.
Every warrior answered to his name. War dances
were indulged in within sight of the camp of the
troops, and great was the confidence of the savages
that they could stand off their enemies indefinitely.
In the soldiers' camp everyone was busy attending
to the wounded. Many of the Indians had managed
to secure the weapons of the soldiers who had been
killed, which were far superior to their own. They
also found much ammunition scattered over the
ground where the soldiers had retreated. There were
no sad-hearted braves among Captain Jack's fifty-
two warriors that night.

It was now very plain to General Gillem that the
Modocs were not going to be subdued by ordinary
methods. Troops were rushed to the Lava Beds
from every available point, until there were a thousand soldiers on the ground. Before they could get
into action, however, word was received from Washington instructing that a Peace Commission be
formed to treat with the savages. The members of
this commission were Gen. E. R. S. Canby, Rev. E.
Thomas, Col. A. B. Meacham, and L. S. Dyer. Cap-

tain Jack agreed to meet the Commissioners at Fairchild's ranch on the 10th of March, 1873, and in
company with several of his head fighting men,
among whom were Boston Charley, Bogus Charley,
Hooker Jim and Dave Rock, he met the Commissioners as agreed.   Frank Riddle and his wife,
Tobey, again acted as interpreters.   No decision was
reached at the first day's council.   It was very plain
to the Commissioners, however, that the Indians
were not going to agree on a peace unless their
wishes were, in a measure, respected regarding the
land upon which they were to be placed.

Another meeting was planned for the 27th, at
which it was hoped an agreement could be reached.
Captain Jack asked that a reservation be set aside
for his people near Hot Creek, or else near the Fairchild ranch.   This was refused.   Then Jack asked
that the destitute and unfertile Lava Beds be given
to his people, "as no white man would ever want to
live in such a barren spot."   To this the Commissioners replied that nothing could be granted "until
peace was first made."   Jack was insistent that "a
home be given to us in this country."   To this General Canby retorted, "We cannot make you that
promise; you and the whites could not get along."
The Commissioners told the Indians that they must
come under the white man's law, and General Canby
insisted that the Modocs come out from their stronghold under a flag of truce.   To this Jack scornfully
answered:

"Look here, Canby, when I was a boy a man
named Ben Wright called forty-five of my people
out under a flag of truce.   How many of them do you

think got away with their lives? Just seven of
them. I will not come out under a flag of truce,
I dare not do it."

Nothing was gained at this council. Neither side
would yield to the other. After the Commissioners
had departed the Modocs went to their stronghold
and held a council of war. They were greatly
wrought up over the refusal of the Commissioners
to grant them a home in the country where they and
their people had always lived. Black Jim, one of the
warriors, made a motion that the Commissioners be
killed at the next peace talk. About fifteen of the
braves sided with him. Captain Jack would not
agree to anything of the sort, insisting that he would
yet make the Commissioners yield to him by sticking
to his point, and that he would yet get his people
the land they desired for a reservation. "All I ask
is that you people be patient and behave yourselves
and wait," he pleaded. "I do not want to do anything rash; that will never do."

But now others of the Modocs sided with Black
Jim and refused to yield to their chief. They taunted
him with being "an old woman." A dozen of his
warriors told him his advice was not good. "Let us
take the advice of Black Jim," they urged. "We
are doomed anyway. Let us fight and die like true
Modocs."

Captain Jack was called a coward and a squaw,
and in derision one of the warriors threw a shawl
over his shoulders and a squaw's hat was forced on
his head. This enraged the chief, and he declared
he would show them that he was a true Modoc. It
was thereupon decided — much against the advice

and pleading of Captain Jack — to massacre the Commissioners at the next peace talk, and the chief was elected to kill General Canby, while certain others were delegated to murder the other Commissioners.

For two days Captain Jack brooded over his promise to assist in the cowardly work. Then he asked that he be allowed to withdraw. "Do not hold me to this," he urged. "I ask you this for the love I hold for you all. If we go ahead with this work we are all doomed." Angrily the warriors insisted that the chief play the part delegated to him.

On the 8th of April Tobey Riddle was sent by the Commissioners to Captain Jack's camp with a message that they desired to have another talk with the Indians. They wanted Jack to meet them with five of his men, unarmed, agreeing themselves to likewise attend the council without weapons. Jack sent back word that he and his men would come. On the return of Tobey Riddle to the camp of the Commissioners, she was overtaken by William Faithful, one of the Modoc braves, who was, moreover, a cousin of Tobey. He warned the Modoc woman of the decision of the savages to murder the Commissioners at the next peace talk, and urged her to have them stay away. Greatly alarmed, Tobey at once sought her husband and General Canby, to whom she imparted the danger. The general at once called together the other members of the Commission, and told them of the impending peril. None would believe it. General Canby was skeptical. "What!" he exclaimed, "a mere half dozen Indians murder us

right under the very noses of a thousand troops?
Impossible! They cannot and dare not do it."

Said the Rev. Thomas: "God will not let them do
such a dreadful thing. I trust in God to protect us."

Then Frank Riddle spoke up. "Gentlemen," he
said seriously, "I have known these Modocs many
years, and if they have decided to murder you Commissioners, they will do it. I know it. If you go to
meet them, you will never see the sun rise in this
world again. I know my wife is telling you the
truth."

Colonel Meacham and L. S. Dyer, the two others
of the Commission, agreed with Riddle. They had
no faith in the Modocs at all, after the warning just
given by Tobey Riddle.

The matter thus rested for the night. In the
morning Riddle and his wife renewed their pleading
with the Commissioners not to go to the meeting.
With tears streaming down her face, Tobey besought
them to listen to her warning, and heed the advice
of her husband and herself. Soon after, Captain
Jack sent word from his stronghold that he would
not be able to meet the Commissioners that day, but
wished to see Tobey Riddle alone. She at once
mounted her horse and rode over into the Indian
camp, where Captain Jack instructed her to tell the
Commissioners to be at the peace tent, situated half-
way between the Indian camp and that of the soldiers, early the following morning. "Tell them we
will be there, six of us, unarmed, and nothing will
happen if they talk sense to us."

To assume friendship, four of the Modoc braves
accompanied Tobey back to the camp of the Com-

missioners, where they were invited to remain to
dinner, and where, to all appearances, they were on
the best terms of friendship. After the departure
of the Indians, Tobey Riddle again pleaded with
General Canby not to go to the meeting. "Just as
sure as you go, you will all be brought back here
cut to pieces," she warned.

The following morning the Commissioners once
more asked Riddle if he really thought there was
danger in attending the meeting. He replied with
considerable emphasis, "As I told you gentlemen
yesterday, you will certainly be killed if you go."

General Canby laughed, and in bantering tones
he bade his brother officers goodby "in case I never
return," as he picked up a box of cigars and started
toward the council tent, half a mile distant, closely
followed by Dr. Thomas. All of the Commissioners
had been urged to secrete revolvers on their persons,
and Meacham and Dyer each placed a small Der-
ringer pistol in their pockets. But the others pos-
itively refused to go armed, for the reason that they
had given their word to the Modocs to come unarmed, and they would not break their promise.
Riddle and his wife, although both believed they
would be massacred with the others, bravely and
resolutely determined to accompany the Commissioners to act in their regular capacity as interpreters.

When the members were all assembled at the
council tent, they found Captain Jack and his five
braves already there. It was seen at a glance, however, that the Modocs had broken their promise
about coming unarmed, as the butts of revolvers

protruded from the pockets of each. The Commissioners, however, determined to face the ordeal. Those present at the council were as follows: Of the whites, General Canby, Rev. Thomas, Col. Meacham, L. S. Dyer, Frank Riddle and his wife, Tobey. The Modocs were represented by Captain Jack, John Sconchin, Boston Charley, Bogus Charley, Black Jim and Hooker Jim.

After shaking hands all around, General Canby opened the box of cigars and passed them around to the Indians. The council then opened. The speech-making lasted nearly an hour, neither side being able to arrive at a decision. The Modocs, however, grew more bold and insolent in their demands, and the Commissioners soon realized that serious trouble was imminent. At this point, Captain Jack withdrew from the council for a moment or two, but soon returned, just as General Canby arose to speak. As he was addressing the Indians very earnestly, two Modocs not in the council suddenly appeared from behind some large rocks, each with several rifles in his arms.

At this juncture Captain Jack drew his revolver, exclaiming in the Modoc tongue, "All ready!" Pointing the weapon full in Canby's face, he pulled the trigger, but the weapon failed to explode. He quickly drew the hammer back again and snapped it. There was a loud report, and the bullet struck the brave old general directly under the right eye. He reeled and started to run, but was tripped, thrown to the ground and his throat cut by Bogus Charley. At the same time Boston Charley shot Dr. Thomas, who fell to the ground, exclaiming:

"Don't shoot me again, Charley, I am a dead man!"

"Damn you," retorted Boston, "mebby nex' time you b'leev what squaw tell you, eh?" He then shot the dying man again and again until life was extinct.

Meacham was also shot about the same time as the others. Sconchin did the shooting. Tobey Riddle sprang forward, and with the strength of a wild beast, struck the Indian again and again, finally knocking him down; but Sconchin arose and knocked Tobey down. He then shot Meacham seven times until he was supposed to be dead. Boston Charley then placed his foot on Meacham's neck and started to scalp him. He had already made a long cut in the wounded man's head and started to tear off his scalp, when Tobey Riddle again attacked Meacham's assailants with the ferocity of a tiger, fighting them off, at the same time screaming, "Soldiers are coming!" The Modocs at once fled to their stronghold, leaving Tobey in full possession of the field.

Both Dyer and Riddle jumped to their feet and ran at the first fire. A brave named Shacknasty Jim, who had brought some of the guns from behind the rocks, took after Riddle, emptying his rifle and six-shooter at the fleeing man without effect. Jim thereupon gave up the pursuit. Hooker Jim took after Dyer, shooting at him several times without effect, but after a chase of about four hundred yards, the Indian was outrun, and Dyer and Riddle both reached the camp of the soldiers unharmed.

Tobey Riddle was not further molested. There was not a soldier in sight coming to the rescue of the Commissioners. The brave Modoc woman examined the bodies of Canby and Thomas, finding both dead; but Meacham yet breathed. She placed her saddle blankets under him, mounted her horse and started on the run for the camp to get help. Half way there she met her husband returning with a detachment of soldiers. Meacham was yet alive. He was rushed to the hospital tent on a stretcher. His wounds, while serious, were not necessarily fatal, the surgeons said. Tobey Riddle at once insisted upon nursing him and her plea was granted. In two weeks he was able to sit up, and by the third week was sent to his home in Salem, Oregon, where he eventually recovered.

After the killing of the Commissioners there was no more fighting for three days. Then the soldiers again advanced on the Modoc stronghold. They were met by a withering fire which killed seven or eight soldiers. Not an Indian was even wounded in the three days' fighting which followed. Shells and bullet fire both were used against the Modoc stronghold without any apparent effect. Nothing could penetrate the craggy fastnesses and rocky walls which surrounded the Modocs, and it was sure death every time the soldiers charged. This was amply demonstrated time and again. Not an Indian could the troops see. The best they could do was to watch for a puff of smoke and fire at that. The Indians now had plenty of guns and ammunition which they had secured from the dead soldiers, but provisions were running low. There were about 150 mouths to feed, besides the fighting braves, and the warriors were hampered and handicapped thereby.

For some days the fighting continued, but it was

soon agreed by the Indians that they could not hope to much longer continue the siege. Their women and children and the old people were in constant danger, and at last it was decided to evacuate the Lava Beds in the night. It was to be every man for himself.

The next day when the soldiers advanced, they found the stronghold deserted, save for four old blind and crippled Modocs, who were promptly shot down. While searching for the trail of the departed braves, a volley was fired at the troops from ambush which was so deadly that twenty-two soldiers were instantly killed and eighteen wounded. There were but twenty-one Indians in this attacking party, many of them now being armed with Spencer repeating rifles secured from the soldiers. Not an Indian was struck by a bullet fired by the troops. After the battle a wounded soldier, left on the field, shot and killed one of the Modoc known as "Little Ike." This soldier was hunted down and shot several times by the Modocs, being left for dead on the field. He was later rescued by the troops, but died in the hospital.

Following this skirmish, the Modocs had many fights with the soldiers. Along in May, one of the Modocs named "Ellen's Man" was killed, supposedly by soldiers. He was one of the most beloved of the warriors, and a violent quarrel broke out among the band as to the cause of his death. This at last resulted in a division of the fighting forces of the Modocs. One faction, embracing Bogus Charley, Hooker Jim, Scarfaced Charley and Shacknasty Jim, finally went to the Fairchild ranch, where General Davis—then in charge of the troops—was stationed.

They told him they were tired of fighting and wanted to surrender. They also intimated that they were ready and willing to assist the troops in running down the remainder of Captain Jack's warriors. General Davis at once engaged the traitors as scouts and trailers at salaries of $100 each per month.

It was hard dodging for Captain Jack after that. However, he and his small band managed to elude the troops until June 1, 1873, when the Modoc warriors who had turned against their chief, trailed him down, and he was captured. With him at the time were his sub-chief, John Sconchin and some forty or fifty others — old men, women and children.

After the capture of Captain Jack had been effected, the prisoners were all removed to Fort Klamath, Oregon. Here the leading members of the band stood trial for murder. These were Captain Jack, John Sconchin, Boston Charley, Black Jim and Slolux. The four Modoc traitors who had assisted in the murder of General Canby and Rev. Thomas, were freed — or rather not tried at all for complicity in the massacre, from the fact that they had surrendered voluntarily and rendered valuable aid in running down the remnants of the band. The trial began in July and lasted nearly a month. Every Modoc Indian was placed on the stand, but they had no counsel. Frank and Tobey Riddle acted as interpreters during the entire trial, rendering invaluable service.

When Captain Jack was put on the stand he made a masterly talk. In ringing terms he scathingly denounced the treatment of his tribe at the hands of

the whites and the government. Among other things
he said:

"The government ought to care for my young people. See the good land and the size of the country
that is taken away from me and my people. If I
wanted to talk more I could tell you facts, and prove
by white people that which would open your eyes
about the way my people have been murdered by the
whites. I will say that not one white man was ever
punished for those deeds. If the white people who
killed our women and children had been tried and
punished, I would not have thought so much about
myself and my companions. Do we Indians stand
any show for justice with you white people and
your own laws? I say no! You white people can
shoot any of us Indians any time you want to,
whether we are at war or at peace. Can any of you
tell me whenever any white man has been punished
in the past for killing a Modoc in cold blood? No, you
cannot tell me! I am on the edge of the grave. My
life is in you people's hands. I charge the white
people with wholesale murder — not only once, but
many times. Think about Ben Wright — what did
he do? He killed nearly fifty of my people, among
them my father. Was he or any of his men ever
punished? No, not one! Mind you, Ben Wright
and his men were civilized white people. The other
whites at Yreka made a hero of him because he murdered innocent Indians. Now, here I am. I killed
one man after I had been fooled by him many times,
and I was forced to do the act by my own warriors.
The law says, 'Hang him; he is nothing but an Indian anyhow; we can kill them any time for nothing,

but this one has done something, so hang him.' Why did not the white man's law say that about Ben Wright?"

When the trial ended, four of the Modocs— Captain Jack, Black Jim, Sconchin and Boston Charley —were condemned to hang. Two others—Boncho and Slolux, the Modocs who had brought the guns to the others, were sent to the penitentiary for life. Boncho died at the prison on Alcatraz Island, May 28, 1875.

The hanging of Captain Jack and his three braves took place at Fort Klamath on October 3, 1873. The balance of the tribe were sent to Quapaw Agency in the Indian Territory (now Oklahoma) where in a few years nearly all the older people died, as the climate did not agree with them there. The remnant of the Modoc tribe is now living on the Klamath reservation in Oregon, a bill having been passed some years ago that the descendants of Captain Jack's band should be restored to the rolls of the Klamath Agency, with the privilege of removing there.

There Tobey Riddle lived, and there she died in the latter part of February, 1920. For many, many years she acted as a teacher and missionary to her own race, and was the means of pointing them to the white man's road. In 1875 she made a trip to the East, and saw for the first time the power and prestige of the white people. Tobey Riddle's son, Jeff C. Riddle, now lives at Beatty, Oregon, where he has raised a large family and is highly respected.

It would seem that the State of Oregon should recognize in Tobey Riddle a heroine who should be-

come as well known in American history as Poca-
hontas or Sacajawea, the little Indian guide of Lewis
and Clark. It was not until seventeen years after
the Modoc war that Congress granted this noble Indian woman the slight pittance of $25 per month,
which she received during the balance of her life,
although it would seem that this estimation of her
services to her country should have been recognized
and rewarded at the time her valorous deed was
performed; but no "back pay" was ever granted her.
A monument to her memory is now the most fitting
memorial that the State of Oregon could erect over
her grave.

CHAPTER VI

JIM BRIDGER, GREATEST OF PLAINSMEN

HAD MANY IMITATORS, BUT NO PEERS — HEAD AND SHOULDERS ABOVE OTHER SO-CALLED SCOUTS, GUIDES AND TRAPPERS

I N the years between 1825 and 1870, the West harbored a class of men of a caliber, courage, determination, pluck, fortitude and bravery whose like has never since been seen. These were the trail-blazers — the men who, with rifle and pack, wandered far from the confines of civilization into an entirely unknown and uninhabited wilderness. With no knowledge of the country into which they ventured, save what they learned from the Indian tribes infesting the same, they fared forth in their quest for adventure and fur — and there was plenty of both to be had at that early day.

These men were hardy, bold, fearless and self-reliant — men "with the bark on," if you please. They were familiar with every phase of the rough, out-of-door life they had chosen; no obstacle was too great for them to surmount; no stream too dangerous for them to cross; no mountain too steep for them to scale; no section of the country too wild for them to refuse to penetrate its depths. In fact, the wilder and more dangerous the country, the more eager they were to venture into it, with the spirit of adventure luring them on.

Among these hardy, self-reliant plainsmen and mountaineers was one who stood unrivaled. And yet, he was the most modest, quietest, unassuming frontiersman of his time. His name was James Bridger, or, as he was more affectionately and familiarly called, "Old Jim" Bridger. The name and fame of this greatest of plainsmen will go down into the history of the West, and he will be revered and honored, long after the lesser lights of frontier history are forgotten.

Just as there is "only one Niagara," so there was only one Jim Bridger. Born in Richmond, Virginia, March 17, 1804, he soon left that part of the country with his parents, who emigrated to St. Louis when the boy, Jim, was but eight years of age. There were three children in the family; the mother died in 1816 and the father the following year. Jim Bridger's brother also passed away at an early age, leaving him the care of a younger sister, and for a boy of thirteen this was no small task.

Bridger, shortly thereafter, started in to learn the blacksmith trade, at which he worked until the adventurous spirit locked up in his bosom asserted itself, and in 1822 he joined a band of trappers under command of Gen. Wm. H. Ashley, who were bound for the fur-bearing section of the Rocky Mountains. Here Bridger found himself in his element at last, and he took to the rough life of a trapper with the zeal and earnestness which soon attracted the attention of his older and more experienced companions, all of whom predicted that young Jim Bridger would some day become renowned as a trapper and rifle shot.

The Ashley party were under the direct command of Andrew Henry. On their way into the fur-bearing country, they encountered one misfortune after another. One of their boats, loaded with goods intended for barter with the Indians, was upset, en route up the Missouri River, entailing a loss of some $10,000; their horses were stolen, and the party were so crippled that they were compelled to halt near the mouth of the Yellowstone and "fort up" for the winter. In this wilderness they hunted and trapped, making explorations into the surrounding country, until the spring of 1823.

During the ensuing seven years, Jim Bridger underwent the usual rigorous life of a frontiersman, developing into a keen, shrewd, courageous character, an unerring rifle shot, a trapper of wonderful renown, and an Indian fighter whose name was quickly spread through the camps of the Blackfeet — then the most warlike of the tribes in the Rocky Mountain section — as a "holy terror." It is to be greatly regretted that there is so little actually known of Bridger's wanderings in this period, as he had but little or no education, and could neither read nor write, and therefore kept no diary or journal of his meanderings.

It was during this period of his wanderings — probably about 1824 or 1825, that Bridger first saw Great Salt Lake, being, so far as is known, the first white man to gaze upon this vast body of water. He thought — noting that the water was salt — that he had discovered an arm of the Pacific Ocean, but upon

FORT BRIDGER.   PHOTO TAKEN BY MERRILL BRININSTOOL IN 1924.

(162)

making a tour of observation, it was discovered that the body of water had no outlet.

In 1830 Bridger had become so proficient in his calling and was considered so competent by the Rocky Mountain Fur Company, that he was sent with two hundred men on a side scout for fur into the Big Horn Basin country, when the party crossed the Yellowstone River and went north to about the present site of Great Falls, Montana. It is claimed that it was on this trip that Bridger first saw the Yellowstone Park section.

The wonders of that marvelous region created such an impression upon Bridger that when he began to tell about the beauties and the almost-supernatural features of it, he was not believed. His stories of hot water spouting hundreds of feet into the air, of boiling pools of water within a few feet of pools of ice cold water, and all the other wonderful features which are today one of our greatest tourist attractions, were not believed by his companions, and "Jim Bridger's lies," as they were dubbed, were soon the talk in every trapper's camp. This so angered Bridger that in disgust he began to invent "real whoppers." He declared that one day while out hunting he saw a fine elk feeding apparently a couple of hundred yards away. Being out of meat, he drew up his gun, took careful aim and fired. To his astonishment, the animal did not move nor pay any attention to the discharge of his rifle. Unable to account for such poor shooting, he again took more careful aim and fired. Still the elk remained undisturbed. Bridger thereupon started on a run toward the animal, when, to his astonishment, he plunged slap up against a solid mass of clear, transparent glass, hundreds of feet in height, and it developed that he had been gazing at the elk on the opposite side of this glass mountain, several miles distant, instead of the few hundred feet which he supposed! Today this "glass mountain" is known as the "Obsidian Cliff," one of the great natural features of Yellowstone Park.

Another one of Bridger's yarns was his "sure 'nuff idee" as to why ice cold water dropped into a pool where it instantly became boiling hot. He declared this was due to the friction produced by the rapid descent of the stream over the rocks!

Bridger tried to have the wonders of the Yellowstone exploited, but could get no eastern newspaper editor to take any stock in his "wild-eyed yarns." It is said that the editor of the Kansas City Journal stated editorially in 1879 that Bridger had told him of these wonders fully thirty years before, and that he had really prepared an article for publication, but finally decided against it, fearing the ridicule to which he would be subjected if he printed any of "Jim Bridger's lies."

In spite of the fact that Bridger talked about this wonderful region to everyone he met, he was simply laughed at, called "just a little off," and unmercifully ridiculed; nor was it until nearly 1870 that any specific exploration was made to determine the accuracy of Bridger's report — all of which was found to be literally true. Bridger had described it as a place "where hell literally bubbled up!" Such, indeed, is the Yellowstone Park section of today.

It is now well known that park visitors can

catch trout in an ice cold stream, and without moving from their tracks can swing the fish about into
a boiling pool.   This was one of the stories which
Bridger had so vehemently declared to be an actual
fact.   Yet he was mocked, derided and branded a
liar of the first water!

One of the great natural wonders along the Sweetwater River, Wyoming, is the famous Independence
Rock, a vast formation lying in a perfectly open
country.   Just how this great rock — nearly a mile
in circumference and about 100 feet in height, came
to be placed there, is best told by Bridger: "That
'ere rock, when I fust come into this country, was
jest a pebble on t'other side of the Sweetwater which
I picked up one day and threw over to this side, and
the soil is so derned prolific that it grew into this
yere rock."

In one of Bridger's Indian battles in the Blackfoot country, he was wounded in the back by an
arrow, the iron point of which remained firmly im-
bedded in the flesh for nearly three years.   It was
finally removed by Dr. Marcus Whitman, the noted
Oregon missionary, at that time en route to his station, and who fell in with Bridger and his party at
the annual rendezvous of the trappers in 1835 at
Pierre's Hole.   No anesthetic was administered during the operation, and speedy relief was afforded
from the extraction of the iron arrow point, which
was nearly three inches in length.

A huge volume could be written detailing the
numerous adventures and hair-breadth escapes from
savages and wild animals, through which Jim Bridger passed during his years on the frontier as a

trapper and mountain man. He often declared, when one of his friends was detailing to him the marvelous yarns of Baron Munchausen, that "some of his own adventures would sound jest as reliable if writ into a book."

The historic Fort Bridger, located on Black's Fork of the Green River, was erected by Bridger in 1843, and this point became a most noted one during the years of overland travel to the Pacific Coast states. The old Mormon Trail was close by, and the North and South Platte routes met near Fort Bridger, hence, the place became well known. Here Bridger's skill as a blacksmith — which had long laid dormant — came into play. He opened a shop, supply store and trading post, and as the overland travel was heavy, he soon had more work on hand than he could possibly attend to. Most of the emigrants were fairly well supplied with money, and of course, had to buy provisions and supplies, and have their animals shod and their wagons looked over about the time they reached Bridger's post. As these transactions were mostly cash, Bridger soon acquired considerable money, and he did a lively business, although doubtless he did not spend all his time at Bridger's Fort, as history records that he made various trapping excursions into the mountains from time to time. However, Fort Bridger soon came to be looked upon as a veritable oasis in the desert, and he certainly exercised good judgment in locating his post at such a favorable spot.

By 1857, however, overland travel had dropped off considerably from what it had been in previous years, and Bridger leased his property to the United

JAMES BRIDGER
1804 1881
CELEBRATED AS A HUNTER, TRAPPER,
FUR TRADER AND GUIDE. DISCOVERED
GREAT SALT LAKE 1824, THE SOUTH
PASS 1827. VISITED YELLOWSTONE LAKE
AND GEYSERS 1830. FOUNDED FT. BRIDGER
1843. OPENED OVERLAND ROUTE BY
BRIDGER'S PASS TO GREAT SALT LAKE.
WAS GUIDE FOR U.S. EXPLORING
EXPEDITIONS, ALBERT SIDNEY JOHNSTON'S
ARMY IN 1857, AND G.M. DODGE IN U.P.
SURVEYS AND INDIAN CAMPAIGNS 1865-66.
THIS MONUMENT IS ERECTED AS A
TRIBUTE TO HIS PIONEER WORK BY
MAJ. GEN. G.M. DODGE

THE BRIDGER MONUMENT IN MT. WASHINGTON CEMETERY, KANSAS CITY, MO., ERECTED BY GEN. GRENVILLE DODGE, BUILDER OF THE UNION PACIFIC RY. PHOTO COURTESY DAVISON, KANSAS CITY, MO.

States government for the sum of $600 per year. Uncle Sam never paid him a cent, however, and it was not until thirty years later that the government finally allowed him $6,000 for the improvements he had made to the property, but not a cent for the land itself!

Passing over many eventful years in the life of Bridger we find him, in 1866, in the capacity of guide for Col. Henry B. Carrington's expedition sent into what is now the present state of Wyoming, for the purpose of building forts and protecting the emigrants who were bound for the Montana gold fields and points on the Pacific Coast. Carrington left Fort Kearney, Nebraska, May 19, 1866, under orders to enter the Powder River and Big Horn countries and build three forts. This was invading the very cream of what was then the hunting grounds of the Sioux — their last and best game section.

The Carrington expedition was decidedly obnoxious to Red Cloud, the great war chief of the Sioux, who declared in a conference held at Fort Laramie, in June, 1866, that while he would not object to the government retaining Fort Reno along the Bozeman Trail, under no circumstances whatever would he allow the soldiers to penetrate further north into his hunting country, but that he "would kill every soldier or white man who went north of Crazy Woman's Fork."

At this conference, Jim Bridger was an attentive spectator and listener. He sat on a low seat with his elbows on his knees and his chin buried in his hands, watching every movement and listening to every fiery word which dropped from the lips of Red

Cloud, who bitterly declared that "the Great Father had sent soldiers to steal the road, whether the Indian said yes or no." And when Red Cloud, with head erect and eye flashing fire, stalked haughtily out of the council, refusing to shake hands with any of the assembled government representatives, Bridger shook his head and declared "hell would soon be a-poppin'."

Bridger was right. No sooner had Carrington reached the point north of Fort Reno where he determined to commence the erection of the second fort, than "hell was a-poppin'" for sure. Scarcely a day passed during the erection of the fort, but that skirmishes with the Indians occurred. In fact, during the two years of its existence, Fort Phil Kearney witnessed more than fifty distinct skirmishes and fights with the Sioux in the immediate vicinity of the post. The terrible Fetterman disaster of December 21, 1866, when eighty-one men were drawn into an ambush and slaughtered to a man, was only one object lesson drawn by the wily Red Cloud, who was probably the greatest Indian general of any tribe.

During most of these troubles Jim Bridger was acting as post scout for Col. Carrington, who had, meantime, sent a detachment further north to erect the third fort which was to serve as protection along the Bozeman Trail. This post was known as Fort C. F. Smith, and was built on the Big Horn River.

During the time of bitterest trial at Fort Phil Kearney, Jim Bridger was a source of the greatest comfort to the women and children of the post, to all of whom he was a faithful friend and adviser.

His devotion and willingness to cheer them were greatly prized, and he was the one man in whom all placed implicit trust. No man was so keenly alive to the dangers about them; none so well knew Indian wiles and warfare, and none so instinctively seemed to know the invisible as well as the visible operations of the Sioux.

In August, 1868, the dangers along the Bozeman Trail had become such that the government determined to evacuate the country. This was exactly what Red Cloud was playing for. In vain had the government attempted to get him to listen to its appeals that a wagon road be opened into the Montana country. His only ultimatum was that the government abandon the forts and take every soldier out of the country — and Uncle Sam at length was compelled to listen to the great chief. The country was abandoned, the forts evacuated and the Indians immediately burned the hated military posts to the ground.

Much more could be said of Bridger's great value to the government. No important military expeditions were planned without employing him to guide them whenever possible. He was greatly respected and revered by all the old time army officers, who paid the great frontiersman marked deference. Even the Indians regarded him with awe and wonder, and feared the magic power which he seemed to hold over them. And through it all he remained the same simple-hearted, unpretentious, plain prairie-man, who hated sham and braggadocio and detested anything which smacked of self-praise.

But the greatest injustice ever done Jim Bridger

and his fame and reputation, is that which is shown in a moving picture film entitled, "The Covered Wagon." In this picture Bridger is represented as a whisky-soaked, sodden, blear-eyed old sot who cannot make a move of any consequence nor remember past events, unless he is filled to the brim with liquor. While Bridger doubtless liked his "toddy," in common with most of the mountain-men of his day and time, it is an indisputable fact that he was anything but a confirmed drunkard. It stands to reason that had he been such, the United States Government never would have employed him as a guide in its most noted expeditions, nor would Bridger have been respected and revered by all classes of men on the frontier — as he most certainly was. It is libel of the most underhanded sort, and places this grand old pioneer in a position which should call forth an indignant protest from those, at least, who are familiar with Bridger's history, his past life and his valuable services to the United States Government. A daughter of Bridger's — Mrs. Virginia Bridger Hahn, of Kansas City, Kansas, has filed suit against the makers of "The Covered Wagon" film for thus defaming the character of her illustrious father.

There are several men living today who knew Jim Bridger intimately, among whom are Hon. John Hunton, of Fort Laramie, where Bridger was stationed as post guide in 1868. Mr. Hunton was at that time in the employ of the post sutler at Fort Laramie, and Bridger slept in a bunk in the same room with Mr. Hunton and other employes, with all of whom he was on the most familiar terms.

MAJOR JAMES BRIDGER.

(172)

Dr. Gilbert E. Bailey* of Los Angeles, Cal., head of the chair of geology of the University of Southern California, also knew Bridger intimately, having passed a winter with him in the latter '60's while a member of the surveying party which was putting the Union Pacific Railroad through. Dr. Bailey at that time was a youth of about eighteen, but distinctly recalls the noted frontiersman, who was acting as guide for the party, and whose quiet deportment and simple manners made a lasting impression upon him.

Major A. B. Ostrander, of Seattle, Wash., met and became acquainted with Bridger at old Fort Phil Kearney in 1866. At that time Ostrander was a youth of nineteen, who had left the headquarters of Gen. Philip St. George Cooke in Omaha, where he had been acting as confidential clerk, to join his regiment, the 18th U. S. Infantry, at Fort Phil Kearney. He describes Bridger as a man who would command a second glance from anyone; admired and respected by all his superiors, and of the strictest integrity and honesty, and far from being the drunken sot which "The Covered Wagon" producers would foist on the American public, which public — more shame to them — knows little or nothing of the history of this great frontiersman, and doubtless believed the film-makers were showing up Bridger in his true light.

There are other old timers who knew Bridger well enough to recall that he was not a drunken bum, but a gentleman, even though a diamond in the rough, who could fully and intelligently describe any coun-

---

* Since deceased.

try which he had once seen, and could make a map, showing the streams, mountains and other features absolutely correct, so that there was no trouble following it and fully understanding it.

Bridger never made claims of knowledge of any country over which he had not traveled. In his little pamphlet on the life of Bridger, Gen. Grenville Dodge says:

"He was a good judge of human nature. His comments upon people whom he had met and been with were always intelligent and seldom critical. He always spoke of their good parts, and was universally respected by the mountain-men, and looked upon as a leader also by all the Indians. He was careful to never give his word without fulfilling it. He understood thoroughly the Indian character, their peculiarities and superstitions. He felt keenly any loss of confidence in him or his judgment, especially when acting as guide; and when he struck a country or trail with which he was not familiar, he would frankly say so, but would often say he could take our party up to the point he wanted to reach. As a guide, I do not think he had his equal on the Plains. So remarkable a man should not be lost to history and to his country, and his work allowed to be forgotten."

Bridger married into two different Indian tribes. His first wife was a Ute, by whom he had two children, both of whom were educated in St. Louis. His second wife also was a Ute, by whom he had a daughter, who was likewise sent to school in St. Louis. His third wife was from the Snake tribe. Bridger did not have but one wife at a time, in spite of the representations of "The Covered Wagon" that he employed "Mormon tactics" and had several wives at the same time.

Bridger was 77 years of age when he died, in 1881. He was buried on the Stubbins Watts farm, not far south of Westport, Mo.

In 1902, his friend, Gen. Grenville Dodge, builder of the Union Pacific railroad, learned for the first time where the body of the noted old plainsman lay, and that his grave was neglected and forgotten. Gen. Dodge felt keenly that this celebrated frontier character should be more prominently remembered, and with other admirers he interested the Mount Washington Cemetery Association of Kansas City in his plans, and they donated a prominent and beautiful burial site, where the remains of the noted old pioneer were removed, and on December 11, 1904, an imposing monument was unveiled bearing the following inscription:

1804 — JAMES BRIDGER — 1881

Celebrated as a Hunter, Trapper, Fur Trader and Guide. Discovered Great Salt Lake, 1824; the South Pass, 1827; Visited Yellowstone Lake and Geysers, 1830; Founded Fort Bridger, 1843; Opened Overland Route by Bridger's Pass to Great Salt Lake. Was Guide for Exploring Expeditions, Albert Sidney Johnson's Army, in 1857, and G. M. Dodge in U. P. Surveys and Indian Campaign, 1865-66. This monument is erected as a Tribute to his Pioneer Work by Major General G. M. Dodge.

General Dodge further speaks of Bridger as follows:

"In person he was over six feet tall, spare, straight as an arrow, agile, raw-boned and of powerful frame; eyes gray; hair brown and abundant, even in old age; expression mild and manners agreeable. He was hospitable and generous and was always trusted and respected. He possessed in a high degree the confidence of the Indians. He was one of the most noted hunters and trappers on the Plains. Naturally shrewd and observing, he carefully studied the habits of all wild animals, especially the beaver, and he became one of the most expert of trappers. As a guide he was without an equal, and this is the testimony of everyone who ever employed him. He was a born topographer; the whole West was mapped out in his mind, and such was his instinctive sense of locality and direction, that it used to be said of him that he could *smell* his way where he could not see it. He was a complete master of plains and woodcraft, equal to any emergency, full of resources to overcome any obstacle, and I came to learn how it was that for months such men could live without food except what the country afforded. Nothing escaped the vision of these men — the propping of a stick, the breaking of a twig, the turning of the growing grass, all brought knowledge to them, and they could tell who or what had done it. A single horse or Indian could not cross the trail but that they discovered it, and could tell how long since they passed. Their methods of hunting game were perfect, and we were never out of meat. Herbs, roots, berries, barks of trees and everything that was edible, they knew. They could minister to the sick, dress wounds — in fact, in all my experience I never saw Bridger, nor any of the other voyagers of the plains and mountains, meet any obstacle which they could not overcome."

Such unstinted words of praise from a man who knew Jim Bridger so intimately should be sufficient to prove that this great man — this American — should be placed in the proper niche where he belongs, along with such men as Daniel Boone, Simon Kenton, Davy Crockett, Kit Carson, Uncle Dick Wootton, Lucien Maxwell and other renowned frontier characters.

The author can give Jim Bridger no better "send-off" than the words he quoted in "The Bozeman Trail"* — "Jim Bridger was a true type of the man necessary as a trail-blazer to the great unexplored regions of the mighty West. He had many imitators, but no peers. He was the uncrowned king of all the Rocky Mountain scouts, guides, trailers, trappers, mountain-men and plainsmen between 1830 and 1870."

---

*The "Bozeman Trail" by Hebard and Brininstool, (The A. H. Clark Co.) 1921.

CHAPTER VII

"CALAMITY JANE"

THE MOST UNIQUE, PICTURESQUE, AND ROMANTIC
FIGURE IN BLACK HILLS HISTORY.

"WHO was 'Calamity Jane'?"
This question has been asked so many times by the younger generation — most of whom seem to have little or no real knowledge of the history of the West — that the author feels constrained to give some facts about the most-talked-of frontier woman whose name is linked with border history — and especially the history of Deadwood, South Dakota, and the Black Hills section in general.

"A compound mixture of good and bad," is the way she has been described by old frontier friends who knew Calamity Jane in the Black Hills, from her initial appearance there in 1875 to the day of her death, in 1903.

"She could swear harder, drink more whiskey and raise hell generally more than any individual I ever met in all my days on the frontier," says another old-timer, "and yet the woman had a kind heart, would give her last dollar to anyone in distress, and was known far and wide for her generous, unselfish and chivalrous nature."

There appears to be very little in print really authentic regarding this picturesque and romantic female character of Western history. Her maiden name was Mary (or Martha) Canary.   In a statement made public some years ago, the woman gave some facts regarding her life which may, or may not, be true, but which are substantially as follows:

"My maiden name was Martha Cannary. (note difference in spelling from the generally-accepted version, which is 'Canary.')   I was born in Princeton, Mo., May 1, 1852. My father and mother were natives of Ohio. There were two brothers and three sisters, I being the eldest of these children.

"As a child I was always fond of adventure and out-of-door exercise, having an especial fondness for horses, which I began to ride at an early age, and continued to do so until I became an expert horsewoman, being able to handle the most vicious and stubborn animals. In fact, the greater portion of my life, in early times, was spent in this manner.

"In 1865 we emigrated from our home in Missouri by the Overland route, to Virginia City, Montana. We were five months in making this trip. While on the way, the greater portion of my time was spent in hunting, along with the men and hunters in the party — in fact, I was at all times with men when there was excitement and adventure to be had.

"By the time we reached Virginia City, I was considered a remarkable shot and fearless rider for a girl of my age. I remember many occurrences on the journey from Missouri to Montana. Many times, in crossing the mountains, the condition of the trails was so bad that frequently it was necessary to lower the wagons over ledges by hand, with ropes, for the travel was so rough that horses were of no use in getting across the roughest places.

"We also had many exciting times fording the streams, many of which were notorious for quick-sands and boggy places, where, unless we were very careful, we would have lost horses and all. Then, we had many difficulties to encounter in the way of streams swelling because of heavy rains. Very often, on such occasions, have I mounted my pony and swam the animal across the stream several times, merely to amuse myself. I have had many narrow escapes from being washed away to certain death on such occasions; but as the pioneers of those days had plenty of courage, we overcame all obstacles, and finally reached Virginia City in safety.

"My mother died at Blackfoot, Montana, in 1866, where we buried her. I left Montana in the spring of 1866 for Utah, arriving in Salt Lake City during the summer. I remained in Utah until 1867, where my father died. I then went to Fort Bridger, Wyoming Territory, where I arrived May 1, 1868. I remained around Fort Bridger during 1868, then went to Piedmont, Wyoming, following up the building of the Union Pacific railroad.

"I joined General Custer as a scout at Fort Russell, Wyoming, in 1870, and started for Arizona for the Indian campaign.[1] Up to this time I had always worn the costume of my sex. When I joined Custer

[1] It is very doubtful indeed if Calamity Jane was ever connected with the Seventh Cavalry as a "scout" or in any other capacity, although it is variously stated that she did succeed in getting in with General Crook's columns as a mule-whacker or teamster until her sex was discovered, when she was invariably ordered to "vamoose." She generally wore men's clothing. General Custer took no part in any campaigns against Indians in Arizona.

I donned the uniform of the soldier. It was a bit awkward at first, but I soon got to be perfectly at home in men's clothing.

"I was in Arizona up to the winter of 1871, and during that time I had a great many adventures with Indians, for as a scout, I had a great many dangerous missions to perform; but while I was in many close places, I always succeeded in getting away safely, for at this time I was considered the most reckless and daring rider, and one of the best shots in the Western country.

"After that campaign I returned to Fort Saunders, Wyoming, remaining there until the spring of 1872, when we were ordered out on the Muscleshell outbreak. In that war Generals Custer, Miles, Terry and Crook were all engaged. This campaign lasted until the fall of 1873. It was during this campaign that I was christened 'Calamity Jane,' the facts being substantially as follows:

"It was on Goose Creek, Wyoming, where the town of Sheridan is now located, where this incident occurred. Captain Egan was in command of the post. We were ordered out to quell an uprising of the Indians, and were out several days. We had numerous skirmishes, in which six soldiers were killed and several severely wounded.

"On returning to the post, we were ambushed about a mile and a half from our destination. When fired upon, Captain Egan was shot. I was riding in advance. Upon hearing the firing, I turned in my saddle and noticed that the captain was reeling as though about to fall from his horse. I wheeled my horse and galloped back in all haste to his side, getting there in time to catch him as he was falling. I lifted him on my horse in front of me, and succeeded in getting him safely back to the fort. When Captain Egan recovered, he laughingly remarked, 'I name you Calamity Jane, the heroine of the Plains.' I have borne the name of Calamity Jane up to the present time. (1895).

"We were afterward ordered to Fort Custer, where we arrived in the spring of 1874.[2] Remained around Fort Custer all summer, and were ordered to Fort Russell that fall. Remained there until the spring of 1875. Were then ordered to the Black Hills to protect miners, as that country was controlled by the Sioux Indians, and the Government had to send soldiers to protect the lives of the miners and settlers in that section. We remained there until the fall of 1875, and wintered at Fort Laramie.

"In the spring of 1876 we were ordered north with General Crook to join Generals Miles, Terry and Custer at Big Horn River. During this march I swam the Platte River at Fort Fetterman, as I was bearing an important dispatch. I had a ninety-mile ride to make, and being wet and cold, I contracted a severe illness, and was sent back to Fort Fetterman in an ambulance by General Crook, where I laid in the hospital fourteen days. When able to ride, I started to Fort Laramie, where I met William Hickok, better known as Wild Bill. He and I started for Deadwood, where we arrived about June.

---

[2] Calamity Jane is mistaken regarding Fort Custer. This post was not built until 1877, the year following the battle of the Little Big Horn, in which Custer was killed. There was no other Fort Custer in 1874.

"During the month of June I acted as pony express rider, carrying the United States mail between Deadwood and Custer, a distance of over 50 miles, over one of the roughest trails in the Black Hills country. Many of the riders before me had been held up and robbed of their packages, mail and money.

"It was considered the most dangerous ride in the Hills, but as my reputation as a rider and quick shot was known, I was molested very little, for the Toll Gatherers looked upon me as a good fellow, and they knew I never missed my mark. I made the round trip every two days, which was considered pretty good time in that country. I remained about Deadwood all that summer, visiting all the camps within an area of a hundred miles.

"My friend, Wild Bill, remained in Deadwood during the summer, with the exception of occasional visits to the camps. On the second of August, 1876, while sitting at a gambling table in the Bella Union saloon, in Deadwood, he was shot in the back of the head by the notorious Jack McCall, a desperado. I was in Deadwood at the time, and upon hearing of the killing, made my way at once to the scene of the shooting, and found that my friend had been killed by McCall. I at once started to look for the assassin, and found him at Surdy's butcher shop. I grabbed a meat cleaver and made him throw up his hands. Through the excitement of hearing of Bill's death, I had left my weapons on the post of my bed. McCall was taken to a log cabin and locked up, well secured, as everyone thought; but he got away and was afterward caught at Fagan's ranch on Horse

Creek, on the old Cheyenne road, and was then taken to Yankton, Dakota, where he was tried, sentenced and hung.[3]

"I remained around Deadwood, locating claims, going from camp to camp, until the spring of 1877. One morning I saddled my horse and rode toward Crook City. I had gone about twelve miles from Deadwood, when at the mouth of Whitewood Creek I met the Overland mail, operating between Deadwood and Cheyenne. The horses were on the dead run, and about two hundred yards from the station. Upon looking closely, I saw that they were pursued by Indians. The horses ran to the barn. As they stopped, I rode up alongside the coach and found the driver, John Slaughter, lying face downward in the boot of the stage. He had been shot by the Indians. When the stage reached the station, the Indians hid in the bushes. I removed all the baggage from the stage, except the mail. I then took the driver's seat, and in all haste drove to Deadwood, carrying the six passengers and the dead driver.[4]

"I left Deadwood in the fall of 1877, and went to Bear Butte Creek with the Seventh Cavalry, and

[3] Calamity Jane is sadly mixed in her facts in the foregoing paragraph. McCall was arrested, tried and acquitted the first time by a citizens' committee. He then went to Laramie City, where he openly boasted of having killed Wild Bill. He was again arrested, tried and sentenced to hang, which sentence was carried out at Yankton, Dakota. The statement that Calamity Jane went after McCall with a meat cleaver, is only one other example of the "long bow" she was wont to draw when boasting of her deeds.

[4] This story never has been authenticated and doubtless Calamity is again drawing the "long bow."

during that fall and winter we built Fort Meade and the town of Sturgis.

"In 1878 I left the command and went to Rapid City, putting in the year prospecting. In 1879 I went to Fort Pierre, and drove trains from Rapid City to Fort Pierre for Frank W. Whittle. I later drove teams from Fort Pierre to Sturgis for Fred Evans. This teaming was done with oxen, as they were better fitted than horses, owing to the rough nature of the country.

"In 1881 I went to Wyoming, returning in 1882 to Miles City, Montana, where I took up a ranch on the Yellowstone, raising stock and cattle. I also kept a wayside inn, where the weary traveler could be accommodated with food, drink or trouble, if he looked for it. I left the ranch in 1883, and went to California, going through the state and territories. I reached Ogden the latter part of 1883. I was in San Francisco in 1884. I left San Francisco that summer for Texas, stopping at Fort Yuma, Arizona, the hottest spot in the United States. I stopped at all points of interest until I reached El Paso in the fall.

"While in El Paso I met Mr. Clinton Burke, a native of Texas, whom I married in August, 1885, as I thought I had traveled through life long enough alone, and concluded it was about time to take a partner for the rest of my days. We remained in Texas, leading a quiet home life, until 1889. On October 28, 1887, I became the mother of a girl baby, the very image of its father — that is what he said — but which had the temper of its mother.

"When we left Texas we went to Boulder, Colorado, where we kept a hotel until 1893, after which we traveled through Wyoming, Montana, Idaho, Washington and Oregon, then back to Montana; then to Deadwood, arriving there October 8, 1895, after an absence of seventeen years. My arrival in Deadwood, after an absence of so many years, created quite an excitement among my many friends of the past, to such an extent that a vast number of citizens who had come to Deadwood during my absence, and who had heard so much of Calamity Jane and her adventures of former years, were anxious to see me.

"Among the many whom I met were several gentlemen from Eastern cities, who advised me to allow myself to be placed before the public in such a manner as to give the people of the Eastern cities an opportunity of seeing the woman scout who was made famous by her daring career in the West and the Black Hills.

"An agent of Kohl & Middleton, the celebrated dime museum men, came to Deadwood, through the solicitations of the gentlemen whom I met there, and arrangements were made to place me before the public in this manner.

"My first engagement began in the Palace Museum, Minneapolis, January 10, 1896, under the management of Kohl & Middleton.

"Hoping this little history of my life may interest all readers, I remain, as in the old days,

"Yours,

"MRS. M. BURKE."

(Better known as Calamity Jane)

"CALAMITY JANE," NOTED BLACK HILLS PIONEER CHARACTER OF THE EARLY DAYS. PHOTO COURTESY OF H. R. LOCKE, DEAD-WOOD, S. D.

Thus Calamity Jane gives a hap-hazard and some-what rambling account of her meanderings about the United States during the various years, but having little to say as to her ways and means of support.

In none of the books of Western history, written by men of authority, does the author find any account of Calamity Jane being employed in the regular army as a scout, and it is doubtful, indeed, if she ever did serve in any such capacity, however "mannish" she may have appeared or acted.

Several writers tell of her associating with troops on various campaigns as a mule-skinner or teamster, until her sex was discovered, when she was summarily ordered out of camp. All these reports seem to agree on Jane's ability to drink as much whiskey, chew as rank plug tobacco and swear as blue a streak as any of the rough-and-tough teamsters and mule-whackers with whom she associated.

But there appears to have been another — and better—side to the nature of this strange frontier woman. She was known throughout Deadwood and the surrounding gold camps for her unselfishness, kindness of heart and sympathy in responding to the relief of any sick person — man, woman or child. It is stated by many old-timers of Deadwood that they have known of many instances in which Calamity Jane gave her last dollar to relieve the sufferings of unfortunates who were "down and out."

A story is told that the day "Preacher Smith" arrived in Deadwood, he stood on an empty box in front of Jim Pencil's saloon and began a Biblical discourse to the motley crowd which quickly surrounded him.

He had been addressing his hearers but a brief time before Calamity Jane happened along. Jane was considerably under "the inflooence," and snatching the preacher's old battered hat from his hand, she turned to the crowd and shouted:

"You sinners dig down into your pokes now! This old fellow looks as though he were broke, and I want to collect $200 for him — so limber up, you boys!"

She then started through the crowd, and when she returned to the preacher's "pulpit," she was $235 richer. Emptying it all at the feet of the astonished old sky-pilot, Calamity swaggered off down the street, looking for some new form of excitement.

A friend of the author, George E. Bartlett, who lived in the Black Hills country in its early days, once related that Calamity Jane nursed him through a most serious illness, and that he undoubtedly would have "cashed in" but for her sympathetic ministrations, for which she would accept no remuneration of any sort.

Another old-timer who knew Calamity Jane, and has written some interesting history about her, is Jesse Brown, a pioneer resident of the Black Hills, and one of its best-known and most respected citizens. There seems to be some difference of opinion between Mr. Brown's account of the birthplace of Calamity Jane and that given in her own biography. Mr. Brown states that she was born near Burlington, Iowa, in 1851, while Calamity asserts she first saw the light of day at Princeton, Mo., May 1, 1852. Mr. Brown's account further says that her father was a Baptist minister. Continuing his reminiscence of Calamity, Mr. Brown says:

"It is stated that Jane, in her younger days, was well cared for and trained, but that she was self-willed and full of the joy of life. We first find her running away from home as the mistress of an army lieutenant on one of the expeditions to Wyoming. She later gave birth to a son at Sidney, Nebraska, whom the officer took and sent back east to his parents to raise as a foundling orphan from the plains. The boy was given a good education, and no doubt never knew the truth as to his parentage.

"We again find her in the company of her mother and stepfather, named Hart, a retired regular army officer, crossing the Plains to Salt Lake City, Utah, where they lived for a time. From Salt Lake, Jane ran away to Rawlins, Wyoming. Her stepfather followed her to this place and found that she was at a hotel there, but was informed that she was attending school regularly: This appeared strange to him, as he had been unable to get her to attend school in Utah. However, being assured that the girl was 'going straight,' he returned to his home.

"Soon after this, Jane skipped out to Fort Steele, becoming an inmate of a bawdy house, and quite a pal with teamsters and soldiers. She became expert in tying the diamond hitch and in handling teams, and when an expedition was fitted out to the north, she donned men's attire, and with the aid of her fellow-packers obtained a position as a packer with the government train. In this work she prospered for several months, but when at Hat Creek Station, she and her fellows took an overdose of whisky and went on a wild spree. As a result, the packtrain master discovered her sex and promptly discharged her, and signified his intention of discharging any of the men who were responsible for getting her into the train; but they all kept their secret.

"For a time Calamity Jane was an inmate of a resort in Green River, Wyoming, from which place her brother ran her off at the point of the gun, taking several shots at her by way of good measure. The brother later passed out of notice when the gold rush to the Hills took place. Calamity then wandered from Salt Lake to Blackfoot, Montana, where she presided over a notorious dive known as 'Madam Canary's.'

"Jane was married a number of times — her first husband being named Hunt, and her second, White. White sold out his property and became quite wealthy. He decided to quit the wilderness and rigged his wife out in the finest clothing to be had, and repaired to Denver. A few days of the fancy apparel and classy hotels were enough for the wild, untamed spirit of Martha Jane, and she made her escape. Her husband made search for her, and waited some days for her return, but knowing the spirit of the woman, gave up the search and went his way alone.

"From then on, Calamity Jane became a free lance, roving from town to town and dive to dive, with soldiers, packers, mule-skinners and freighters, as occasion offered. She made her headquarters at Cheyenne, Wyoming. Whenever there was a trip across the Plains, an expedition against the Indians

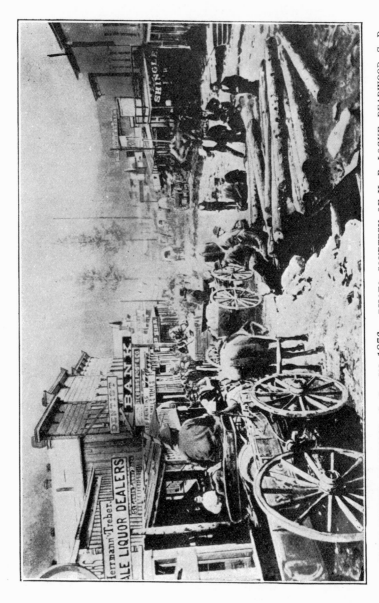

MAIN STREET, DEADWOOD, S. D., IN 1876. PHOTO COURTESY OF H. R. LOCKE, DEADWOOD, S. D.

(192)

or anything to vary the monotony of the small-town life of the West, Jane was on hand, and usually contrived to get away by dressing in male attire, and being smuggled away by her pals.

"On the occasion of General Crook's expedition, she was many miles away from the starting point, but upon hearing of the trip, she hired a team and buggy from a liveryman of Cheyenne, drove rapidly away, smuggled herself in among the soldiers and decamped with them, leaving the liveryman to recover his team and outfit as best he could after placing it in charge of a man at Fort Laramie, where the expedition set out.

"On another occasion she had joined a military expedition and was having the time of her life. When the command halted along the banks of a stream, and the members were enjoying the delights of a cool dip in the waters of the creek, an officer passing by espied the form of Jane splashing about with her fellow-troopers, and the remainder of the journey found her under guard.

"Calamity Jane's introduction to the Black Hills was in 1875, for there we find her dressed as a soldier in the military expedition under General Crook, who, in August, 1875, ordered the miners to leave the Hills until treaties could be made with the Indians. Again she came to the Hills in 1876 with the band in which Wild Bill and Charley Utter were members. However, she was not the consort of Wild Bill, for he was not the kind of a man who was attracted by a woman of Jane's class. Colorado Charley was perhaps her champion, for it is said that he furnished her with a splendid suit of men's buckskin clothing, in which she often appeared.

"No doubt the reader by this time will have concluded that Jane was nothing more than a common prostitute — drunken, disorderly, and wholly devoid of any element or conception of morality. And the question will arise as to how it comes that out of the hundreds, yes, thousands of her fellow-women of the underworld who threw youth, beauty and life itself into the fiery altar of the Molech of passion and immorality, the name of Calamity Jane alone should endure in the annals of time. The answer will be had from the other view of this double-sided woman.

"In 1878 there came a terrible scourge of small-pox among the miners and other residents of Deadwood. Hundreds were prostrated upon their rude beds, and most people were afraid to go near them. Women were few to be had, and they, too, were in fear of their lives. In the hour of terror and death, there came to the front a willing volunteer — the mule-skinning, bull-whacking, rough-and-ready woman from the depths, Calamity Jane! Day and night she went among the sick and dying, and for weeks ministered to their wants, or smoothed the pillow for the dying youth whose mother or sweetheart, perhaps, was waiting and watching for the one who was never to return. It made no difference to her that she knew them not, or that no gold would come to repay her for the labor, the sacrifice or the danger. They were fellow beings in distress — and that was enough for Calamity Jane!

"Another time, while waiting on table in Pierre,

she heard of a family in destitute circumstances, sick with black diphtheria. Neighbors would not go to their aid. Jane had saved up $20 in gold, and proceeding to a grocery she purchased $15 worth of food and medicines and nursed the family until the sickness was over.

"In 1878 the young sister of C. H. Robinson, now sexton of Mount Moriah Cemetery at Deadwood, was sick with typhoid fever. Calamity had known the family for years in Kansas, and she promptly came to their aid, and for two weeks nursed the child until death claimed her as his own.

"Calamity Jane never hesitated to spend her last dollar to aid an unfortunate, and was never backward in asking for money from others to help someone in distress. Her idea of helping others caused her arrest in Deadwood in the early days. It seems that some rough specimen was having what was then known as a 'hell of a time' in one of the resorts of the town in which Jane was an inmate. When he awoke from his drunken slumbers the next day, he found that he was minus some $30, and at once made complaint to the justice of the peace that he had been 'rolled.' Recalling that Jane was there, he charged her with the robbery. She was brought to the bar of the court. When informed of the charge she stated that 'she found the fool drunk under one of the tables.' Searching his pockets she found the money, and realizing that if she did not take it some of the other girls would, she took the cash. The judge then asked her what she had done with it. The reply was that she had given it to the hospital to pay the charges for a young girl who was lying sick

there, without friends or money. The judge
promptly turned her free and scored the sporty
gentleman who was so unwise as to carry money
with him to a dive and expect to carry it away with
him!

"Many other like tales might be added. Calamity
was an expert packer, an able teamster and a crack
rifle shot. She loved the great out-of-doors and the
excitement of the trail. She was the pal of the
men of the fighting line. It is said by E. H. Warren,
of Spearfish that once, while speaking to a pioneer,
a woman came up to the pair, looked them over, and
finally demanded a dollar of the pioneer who, without asking her a question, handed it over to her.
After the woman was gone, the pioneer said: 'That
was Calamity Jane, and as long as I have two dol-
lars in my pocket she can have one of them, for she
saved my life once. We were on a trip, when
Indians opened fire on us and shot my horse from
under me. Jane stopped her horse, grabbed me
by the arm and swung me on behind her and we
escaped.'

"Another time, Calamity and 'Antelope Frank'
were out riding, when Indians appeared and opened
fire upon them. They turned and fled in the direction of the soldiers, but the scout's horse stepped
in a hole, fell and broke its neck, leaving him on
foot. Frank told her to ride on to safety, and that
he would take care of himself, but she said,
'Damned if I will! I will stay right here with you
and we will see how many of those red devils we
can get.' And she did! The pair got into a buffalo wallow and opened fire upon the advancing In-

dians with their rifles and sent them away in retreat, with the loss of five of their number, Jane
having done her share in the execution.

"As time went by and the wild days of the frontier gave way to the more sedate times of later de-
velopment, Jane wandered from town to town, making a living by selling books, photos and receiving
charity from the pioneers. She had a daughter
whom she placed for a time in a Sisters' Convent
when the girl was fourteen years of age.

"Once a kind-hearted woman of wealth from Buffalo, N. Y., sought to lift her out of the slough. She
took Jane back to her home in the distant east. The
lure of the Hills was too strong, however, and Jane
soon bade farewell to the stiff and conventional life
of that section and hastened back to the big-hearted
westerners.

"In physical appearance Jane was a medium-sized
woman, with dark-brown hair and eyes. In her
youth she was of splendid form, clear complexion
and uncommonly good-looking. In her older age
the rough life of the Plains and trails coarsened her
appearance. She could swear like a trooper, drink
like a sailor, and rough it with the roughest. Yet,
when sober, she could do the part of a real lady.
At all times she evinced a great interest in children,
in whose presence she was watchful of her own
conduct.

"She was seen in every town, camp and fort in
the west, and had wandered over all the trails. So
variant were her moods, so many the different incidents of her life, that accordingly there were numerous impressions and ideas of her character. She

was a strange mixture of the wild, untamed individual of the Plains and the mountain trails, and
that of generous, kindly-hearted womanhood. Under
her rough exterior there beat a heart so big and
friendly as to be without measure. Brave, ener-
getic, unfettered, kind, always on the line of action,
with a helping hand ever stretched to aid the poor
and unfortunate, the personality of Calamity Jane
became indelibly stamped upon the minds of the
pioneers.

"The close of the last century found the rover
near to the end of her trail, and in the summer of
1903 she came back to her haunts among the Hills
and told her friends that she was sick and going to
'cash in'. One day she came to a hotel in Terry,
and being sick, asked for a lodging; but the manager
turned her away, thinking her a mere drunk. Soon
after, he learned her identity and took her in; but
dissipation had done its work, and pneumonia made
her an easy victim on August 2, 1903.

"The friends of Calamity took her to the undertaking rooms of C. H. Robinson, at Deadwood.
There, while lying upon the cooling board, numbers
of curious women came to look upon her, and many
clipped locks of hair from her head to the extent
of defacing the remains. 'Smoky Tom,' one of her
early consorts, upon coming to the room and
noticing the work of the vandal hands of the women
(who would have scorned Jane on the streets) pro-
tested against the mutilation, and a wire screen
was placed over Jane's head.

"The pioneers gathered for the funeral, and Rev.
C. B. Clark, of the Methodist church, conducted the

funeral services, assisted by other prominent people of the city. Interment was made in Mount Moriah Cemetery, across the way from the grave of Wild Bill. And fate decreed that C. H. Robinson, whose little sister Calamity Jane had so faithfully watched over in the futile struggle with death, should at last lay her form in the couch of dreamless sleep."

Among men of prominence who were acquainted with the character of Calamity Jane in the old Black Hills days, was Dr. Gilbert E. Bailey, who was for many years at the head of the Chair of Geology in the University of Southern California. Dr. Bailey was at one time State Geologist for Wyoming and had traveled extensively all through the West in his younger days, being a member of the original surveying party of the Union Pacific Railroad. Dr. Bailey was a warm, personal friend of the writer. He died a short time ago in the Southern California metropolis. Under date of September 1, 1923, he wrote:

"My friends in the Black Hills often send me interesting papers, and I enclose one, giving accounts of Calamity Jane's death and funeral, as printed in the Black Hills Pioneer-Times at that time.

"I was well acquainted with the woman, both in Deadwood and at my camp, which she visited several times. I think you could write a good sketch of her life for the benefit of the old-timers.

"She was a woman adventurer with the bark on, as most knew her; but at heart she was very generous and kind-hearted, especially to the sick and those down on their luck.

"If she had been born a man, her life would have attracted very little comment, if any. Being born a woman does not necessarily kill the desire to go and see; but it takes a brave heart to endure the result of following one's desires."

The newspaper alluded to by Dr. Bailey is a copy of the Deadwood Weekly Pioneer-Times of August 3, 1903, and contains the following account of the last days of Calamity Jane in her beloved Black Hills:

"Mrs. Mary E. Burke ('Calamity Jane') female scout, frontier woman, and one of the most picturesque characters of the early West, died at the Calloway Hotel in Terry yesterday afternoon about 5 o'clock, aged 52 years.

"At her request her funeral will be held under the auspices of the early Black Hills settlers, and the remains will be buried in Mount Moriah Cemetery, at Deadwood, beside those of William Hickok (Wild Bill) her former consort, who was murdered in Deadwood in 1876.[5]

"Mrs. Burke arrived in Terry a week ago Friday from Spearfish. She was sick at the time, and to friends she announced that she 'was going to cash in.'

"Calamity Jane's maiden name was Mary E. Canary. Several of the older settlers of Deadwood

---

[5] It is a peculiar coincidence that the death of Calamity Jane should have occurred at almost the same hour of the same day of the same month, 27 years later, as that of Wild Bill Hickok, one of her former friends, and near whom she was buried.

knew her as a little girl in Montana, where her mother was a washerwoman at Blackfoot for a long time.

"The sobriquet 'Calamity Jane' is said to have been applied to her by Bill Nye during the early '70's, when he was editing the Laramie Boomerang.[6]

"She became a rover early in life, and traveled over the country with a number of important expeditions, both military and citizen. She had a rough exterior, but was possessed of a kindly heart and a generous disposition, and many anecdotes are related of her womanly ministrations among the sick and distressed miners, particularly in Deadwood Gulch, at a time when there were but few women in the region, and but for her attentions some of her beneficiaries must have perished.

"She was known to have married a number of times. Her last husband was Clinton Burke, with whom she came to Deadwood in 1895, from Montana. She and Burke separated shortly afterward.

"When she visited Deadwood eight years ago, she had with her a daughter, then fourteen or fifteen years of age, who was placed in school at Sturgis for a short time. Afterwards Mrs. Burke went into a museum in the East, but remained for a short time only, returning to Montana.

"She was then taken up by a lady of Buffalo, N. Y., and induced to accompany her to Buffalo, prom-

---

[6] This is extremely doubtful. There seems to be a difference of opinion as to just how Calamity Jane acquired her nickname. It is also said to have been given her by a sergeant of the Fourteenth Infantry. There seems to be nothing to authenticate any of these stories.

ising her a good home. This proved too tame for
Jane, and she again came West. Since then she
has spent her time in journeying from place to
place, and finally came back to the Black Hills several months ago."

And the curtain falls on the drama of life for
Calamity Jane in the following paragraph under
date of August 5th, 1903, from the Deadwood
Pioneer-Times:

"The remains of Mary E. Burke, the Calamity
Jane of border history, were laid at rest yesterday afternoon. The funeral services were held in
the First Methodist church, and the church was
packed with the old settlers and friends of Calamity.
The funeral sermon was delivered by Dr. C. B.
Clark, and Mrs. M. M. Wheeler and Miss Elsie Sorn-
wall, with Miss Helen Fowler at the organ, furnished the music."

CHAPTER VIII

IN THE DAYS OF THE BUFFALO

HOW THE WORLD'S MOST NUMEROUS GAME ANIMAL
WAS EXTERMINATED.

THE passing of the American bison, commonly
called the buffalo, which roamed the ranges of
Montana and the Middle West in the old days
in countless thousands, is conceded by old plainsmen and army officers of the '60s and '70s to have
been the main solution of the Indian question. In
the early days, when this noble game animal wandered over what was then called "The Great American Desert," the red man placed no dependence
upon the "Great Father" at Washington for food,
shelter and raiment, for it was the buffalo, chiefly,
which furnished him all.

Nearly every part of the body of the buffalo was
utilized, and very little went to waste in an Indian
camp. There was a variety of ways of dressing
the skin of the animal, depending upon the use to
which it was to be put; but the hide itself furnished
the "noble red man" with a lodge and covering to
sleep upon, some of his weapons of war (chiefly
the shield, which was made from the very thick
tough hide of the buffalo's neck), "bull boats" for
crossing the streams, material for his saddle, halters
for his ponies, hair for ornamental purposes, while

many other articles of Indian use came from the skin of this great beast.

When the herds began to be decimated by the ruthless white hide hunters, every part of the flesh of the buffalo found ready use among the Indians. Even the intestines were often eaten raw during the process of butchering and cutting up.

Old-time hunters and trappers all agreed that the flesh of the buffalo, especially that of a young cow or calf — was an ideal meat, and old former buffalo hunters assert that civilized beef was no comparison. Others have contended that it was tough and stringy. Yet other authorities state that many an invalid has gone out on the plains and recovered his health with no shelter but the sky and no food but the flesh of the buffalo.

"Jerked buffalo" was one of the most common of foods in the old plains days. It was cut into very thin strips and hung up in the open air to dry. The pure plains atmosphere was such that the meat cured quickly and would keep indefinitely when thus prepared. Another article of food made by the Indians from the flesh of the buffalo was "pemmican." The thin strips of meat were dried until hard and crisp, after which they were pulverized and mixed with a certain amount of buffalo fat or tallow. This preparation was then packed inside skin bags, sealed tightly and stored away for future use. It is said to have been one of the most nutritious of foods.

In spite of the fact that the plains country was practically treeless, save along the banks of streams, the plainsman of the old days had little or no diffi-

THE AMERICAN BUFFALO, FROM A DRAWING BY IRENE E. THOMPSON.

(205)

culty in procuring plenty of fuel with which to prepare his meals. The dried dung of the buffalo, commonly called "buffalo chips," made a most excellent substitute for wood, and burned readily, with a hot, smokeless flame, and everywhere throughout the buffalo range was found in great quantities, and was always handy.

Although the buffalo was ordinarily not considered pugnacious or dangerous, when wounded this ponderous brute made a most formidable antagonist, and would often turn against its pursuer and disembowel a horse. Buffalo hunting from horseback was considered the peer of all sports in the '70s. Hunting the animal thus was the favorite Indian method of slaughter. Its vision was not keen, and it depended upon its sense of smell to warn it that enemies were near. When great herds of countless thousands of these huge animals were stampeded they turned aside for nothing, but rushed madly along, heedless of anything, often to their own destruction.

The Indian method of hunting was generally by what was termed a "surround." The attack was made under carefully-prepared methods, and attended by the most solemn ceremonial proceedings prior to the hunt. These "surrounds" were scenes of the wildest and most exciting disorder. The buffalo was a difficult animal to kill unless a bullet or arrow pierced the heart.

But it was by the "still-hunting" method that the American bison was practically exterminated by the white man. As the name suggests, the hunter approached his quarry stealthily, under cover as

much as possible, a convenient coulee or ravine
often serving to allow the slayer to approach within
a very short distance of the herd. Unless scented,
the hunter was then ready for the slaughter. The
gun in general use among these hide-hunters was
the old Sharps rifle of .45 and .50 caliber, shooting
from 90 to 125 grains of powder and from 450 to
600 grains of lead. The killer would spread his
loaded shells on the ground, or in his hat, and commence upon the nearest animals. The report of
the rifle seldom alarmed the herd, and as long as
the shooter remained out of sight, it was the next
thing to shooting tame cattle in an open pasture.
When a wounded animal fell, the others would regard their fallen companion in apparent wonder-
ment, and, smelling the blood, they would gather
about the stricken buffalo, often goring and hook-
ing at it, but not understanding its predicament,
apparently thinking it had merely laid down to rest.
Other men who were the "skinners" would come
along later and remove the hides, which were carried to camp, pegged out to dry and then baled for
cartage to the nearest shipping point.

When these hide hunters were exterminating the
herds in the middle '70s, it was nothing unusual for
a single hunter to kill as many as 150 to 200 animals in a day. Little wonder that the Indian vented
his rage against the white man, as he saw his own
doom being sealed by this ruthless, wanton slaughter, taking away the source of his very existence.
It was against the law and in violation of solemn
treaties made with the Indians, who witnessed the
disappearance of their homes, food, clothing, bed-

ding, tepee equipment and everything that satisfied
their wants and needs.   In vain did the Indian
Bureau make a feeble effort to drive the white hide
hunters out.   The men spread all over the Plains
in small parties and slaughtered the buffalo at their
pleasure.

Of the vast numbers of these animals on the
Western Plains between 1850 and 1883 — when the
last big herd was wiped out, statistics differ; but
in the year 1850 it is safe to assume that there
were in the neighborhood of fifty millions of buffalo
ranging between Manitoba and the Staked Plains
of Texas.   Their numbers were literally innumer-
able.   So vast were they that the first railroad trains
on the Union Pacific were often obliged to stop until
the immense herds had crossed their tracks.

In 1871 it was not uncommon to see herds of
buffalo from twenty to fifty miles in width and of
unknown depth from front to rear.   That same
year, Col. Richard Irving Dodge, an army officer
of more than thirty years' experience in Indian warfare, drove in a light wagon along the Arkansas
River, from Walnut Creek to Pawnee Fork, through
one herd of buffalo, not less than 25 miles wide and
of unknown depth, extending as far north and south
as the eye could reach.

In Kansas, the wide expanse of territory lying
south of White Rock Creek and west of the Republican river, was, until 1870, the grazing place
of the "main herd" of buffalo, and from its appearance and location, probably had been for a hundred
years or more.   This scope of country, bounded on
the east by the White Rock, on the southwest by

the Solomon, its interior being traversed by the Limestone, Buffalo, Big Timber and several other smaller streams, also having in its boundary a famous salt marsh, made it a favorite grazing-place for the buffalo.

Either for protection or some other cause, the buffalo, according to old-time hunters, were generally, in the "palmy days" of the slaughter, to be found banded together in large numbers, and after grazing upon the prairie, they would seek a stream for water. In the heat of summer the animals would congregate at the larger streams and stand in the water to protect themselves from insect pests, chief of which was the buffalo gnat. In this manner countless numbers were "bogged down" in quicksand and unable to get back to shore. Shortly after dark the herds would again take to the prairie to graze and rest until the following day, when they would again take to the stream.

While the herd ranging the prairie grazed in an aimless way, and were apparently guided in their movements by the scarcity of forage in one place, or its abundance in another, yet when it came to moving from one grazing ground to another, where the grounds were some distance apart, or when going to a stream, they would always follow an established trail. Many of these old buffalo trails are today plainly discernible.

The buffalo were but little disturbed by the Indians during the spring and summer months, only sufficient to meet their immediate needs being killed. It was not until October, or later, when the fur was in prime condition that the great fall hunt was made

THE HIDE HUNTER AT WORK. FROM A PAINTING BY J. H. MOSER, IN THE NATIONAL MUSEUM.

to secure the winter's supply of meat, as well as hides for tepee covers, clothing, bedding and trading purposes.

It was when the Union Pacific Railroad was being built, in 1869-70 that the real slaughter of the buffalo began. Thousands of men flocked to the Plains to enter this new and novel "industry," and so countless were the hides which were thrown upon the market, that the price dwindled from $4 and $5 each, to as low as a dollar. It was found that buffalo leather, while unfit for making shoes or harness equipment, being too porous, made excellent belting for machinery, and the demand soon became enormous, especially from foreign countries.

At one time, 40,000 buffalo hides were stacked in a corral at Dodge City, Kansas, awaiting shipment. The hide hunters took only the skin, leaving the carcass to rot, while thousands of men — be it said to their disgrace — slaughtered buffalo for the mere wanton pleasure of killing.

Statistics gathered by Major Henry Inman show that from 1868 to 1881, a period of thirteen years, there was paid out, in Kansas alone, $2,500,000 for buffalo bones gathered on the prairies to be utilized by the various carbon works of the country. It required about 100 carcasses to make one ton of bones, the average price paid being about $8 a ton, and the sum mentioned represents the skeletons of over 31,000,000 buffalo!

One night in the early '70's, General Phil Sheridan and Major Inman were occupying the office of Robert M. Wright, a prominent business man of Dodge City—well known to any old Dodge resident. They had just made a trip from Camp Supply, Indian Territory. Mr. Wright was called into the office to consult with the officers as to the probable number of buffalo between Dodge City and Camp Supply, a distance of about 100 miles. Taking a strip fifty miles east and fifty miles west, they had first made an estimate of ten billions. General Sheridan said, "that won't do." They figured awhile longer, and finally made it one billion. Finally they reached the conclusion that there must be 100,000,000, but said they were afraid to give out the figures lest they be accused of prevaricating, but they stated that they believed it nevertheless. This immense herd moved steadily to the North when spring opened, and steadily back to the South when the days began to grow short and winter set in.

The completion of the Western railroad divided the buffalo into two immense herds, known as the Northern and Southern herds. The Southern herd, in 1871, was estimated at 3,000,000, and was being decimated at the rate of from 3,000 to 4,000 a day. Robert Wright and Charles Rath, of Dodge City, shipped over 200,000 buffalo hides the first winter that the Santa Fe Railroad reached Dodge, and they estimated that other parties shipped as many more. Besides these hides, there were 200 cars of hind quarters and two cars of tongues alone shipped!

The Santa Fe Railroad company compiled the following table showing the shipments made over their road, as well as over the Union Pacific and Kansas Pacific. The figures are staggering, but they are absolutely authentic, having been copied from the shipping records.

BUFFALO STATISTICS FOR THE YEARS 1872-73-74

Year	A. T. & S. F. Hides	U. P., K. P. and all Other Railroads Hides	Total
1872	165,721	331,342	497,163
1873	251,443	502,886	754,329
1874	42,289	84,578	126,867
Total........	459,453	918,906	1,378,359
	Meat, lbs.	Meat, lbs.	Total
1872	....	....	....
1873	1,617,600	3,235,200	4,852,800
1874	632,800	1,265,600	1,898,400
Total........	2,250,400	4,500,800	6,751,200
	Bones, lbs.	Bones, lbs.	Total
1872	1,135,300	2,270,600	3,405,900
1873	2,743,100	5,486,200	8,229,300
1874	6,914,950	13,829,900	20,744,850
Total........	10,793,350	21,586,700	32,380,050

Many a Kansas man of those early days, whose crops were gathered in by grasshoppers, drought or a "twister," employed the time between plantings profitably by going out on the prairie with horses and wagons, picking up buffalo bones and hauling them to the nearest railroad station. It was no uncommon sight to see great bone piles half a mile long stacked up along the railroad track, awaiting cars for shipment.

FORTY THOUSAND BUFFALO HIDES IN THE CORRAL OF WRIGHT & RATH, DODGE CITY, KANSAS.

(214)

Robert Wright further states that the buffalo were so plentiful around Dodge City that he used to shoot them from the top of his corral and let the hogs feed upon the carcasses, and that time and again, when putting up hay, it was necessary to have men out day and night to prevent the immense herds of buffalo from mixing in among and stampeding the work cattle and destroying the hay crop.

From 1872 to 1874 it is estimated that there were 1,780,461 buffalo killed and wasted, the meat being left to rot upon the Plains, the hides only being utilized. It is reckoned that 3,158,780 in all were killed by white hunters and the hides shipped over the Santa Fe. During the same period, the Indians killed but 390,000. Besides these, settlers and mountain Indian tribes are estimated to have killed 150,-000, so that the grand total for these years was 3,698,780. During 1876 and 1877, the end came to the great Southern herd, and at the close of the latter year it had been nearly swept from the earth. One hunter in Ford county, Kansas, is credited with having killed 120 buffalo from one stand in forty minutes, and in thirty-five days to have slaughtered 2,173! Another Dodge City man says he killed 1,500 in seven days, and that his greatest killing was 250 in a single day. He employed fifteen skinners, whose sole duty was to follow him up with wagons and remove the hides as fast as he killed the animals.

The great Northern herd went the same way. In 1882 it was estimated that there were 1,000,000 alive in this herd. But there were fully 5,000 white hunters in the field, shooting and slaughtering the beasts at every point. Then came 1883. Thousands more grabbed rifles and took to the field. Such a merciless war of extermination of game animals never was known in any land.

Among the Indians, and even among many of the more superstitious of the old trappers and plainsmen, it was solemnly averred that the buffalo never migrated South, but that the herd which moved Northward every spring was composed of an entirely new band of animals, which had never made the journey before and would never again return to the South. All would admit the Northern migration, but not the Southern. And because the buffalo did not return South in one immense herd, as they did to the North, it was believed they did not go South at all. The Arapahoes, Kiowas and others of the Plains tribes, firmly believed that the buffalo were produced in countless numbers in great caves under the ground, and that every spring the surplus swarmed, like bees from a hive, out of great cave-like openings, and that these caves were located in the Staked Plains of Texas.

This sudden and wanton destruction of the buffalo, which left the Indian virtually a pauper, was unquestionably the chief cause of the later Indian wars on the Plains. Their hunting ground, which the government had sworn by treaty to respect, was overrun with white hunters, settlers, gold-seekers, adventurers and the riff-raff of the plains, who killed off the game without regard to its use or the consequences of such a slaughter to the Indians. The government permitted this invasion of the Indians' hunting grounds, together with the destruction of the game therein, and then expected the untutored, unskilled, ignorant savage to make the sudden change from the chase and the wild, free life to that of the farmer, stock-raiser and agriculturist — a change which the Indian was totally unprepared for and wholly unfitted to make. The very life of the red man was thus destroyed, and he was thrown a pauper on the hands of a set of cold-blooded political parasites, who robbed him first of his sustenance and then his lands. It was only fair that the government, having thus allowed the extermination of the Indian's source of food and raiment, should have immediately prepared proper sustenance for him; but it was not until years later that the Indian received any degree of justice — and let us not boast that this justice, even, has been fair and right to him.

And yet, it had to be! The stern, resistless march of Progress and Civilization was a part of the Great Plan. The West had to be won, and the extermination of the buffalo herds and the subsequent opening of the cattle ranges was the first necessary step.

CHAPTER IX

FREIGHTING ACROSS THE PLAINS

HOW OVERLAND COMMERCE WAS CONDUCTED BEFORE
THE RAILROAD CAME.

D URING the period following the beginning of
the Civil War, it is said that there was not
another section of country on the face of the
globe over which was carried on such an enormous
amount of traffic, using four-footed animals as the
carriers or drawers thereof, as the Plains country
between Atchison, Kansas, and Denver, Colorado.
The Far West was at that time beginning to pour
settlers, adventurers, gold-seekers and other bold
spirits into the new country. Denver was becoming
populous, and all the freight for that section, as well
as for all other portions of the country untouched
by the Missouri river steamboat trade, was necessarily transported by the great "prairie schooners."

Atchison, Kansas, seems to have been the natural
point of overland departure for the Far West because of its superior advantages in many respects.
It had a fine steamboat landing on the Missouri
river, whence all freight from St. Louis — the real
heart of the frontier in those days — was shipped; it
was several miles farther west than any other place
in the state that was favorable for freighting. All
this was a vital point. Every foot of distance
counted, where goods were shipped by the pound.

Further, telegraphic communication with the east was available at Atchison, another decided advantage.

The distance from Atchison to Denver was 620 miles. It was not a cheap proposition to transport goods by freight across the great plains. There was no such thing as classifying goods by the hundredweight, as is done today. Everything went by the pound of sixteen ounces, and the deviation of an ounce or two in the weighing meant considerable to the shipper.

To give the reader an idea of the toll paid in this commerce of the plains, the rate per pound on all merchandise shipped by ox and mule wagon team, from Atchison to Denver, was as follows on the items named: Flour, 9c; tobacco, 12½c; sugar, 13½c; bacon, 15c; dry goods, 15c; crackers, 17c; whisky, 18c; glass, 19½c; trunks, 25c; furniture, 31c. Is it any wonder that some of the freighting outfits waxed rich in those days?

In spite of the tremendous expense attending the shipment of all this enormous amount of merchandise, so great was the volume of business transacted that at times there seemed to be almost one solid line of slow-moving white-topped jolting wagons stretching into limitless space across the Plains. Most of these wagons were drawn by from four to six yoke of oxen, when oxen were used. One authority, who was making a trip from Atchison to Denver by stagecoach, claims to have counted, in one single day's travel, 888 of these huge freighting wagons westward bound, all loaded to the guards with all sorts of merchandise for Denver and adjacent points, and drawn by no less than 10,650 animals!

The time usually required in making a trip from Atchison to Denver was 21 days, when horses or mules were used, and about five weeks when oxen were the transporting power. From eighteen to twenty miles was considered a good day's haul by ox team. While these animals were considerably slower than horses and mules, they were far more dependable and reliable, and they transported the majority of the merchandise which crossed the Plains in the 60's. Mules were usually preferred to horses, being far better able to stand the rigors of the long trip, enduring both hunger and thirst with far less fatigue.

The more experienced of the old-time freighters would choose the ox every time in preference to any other animal, from the fact that he could be relied upon in any emergency, and was far less likely to stampede in case of an attack by Indians.

Very often, where there were goods of a more or less perishable nature to be shipped, these would be carted by horse or mule wagons, as they could make the trip two weeks quicker than oxen. Heavy mining machinery, all forms of hardware stuff, stoves and the like, were sent by the ox teams.

The volume of steamboat traffic done by Atchison in the 60's was immense. It was no rare sight to see from two to four steamers at the levee discharging their cargoes, which were destined to distant military posts or to Denver merchants, while other boats were obliged to wait above and below the levees for their turns. The warehouses were totally inadequate to accommodate the great quantities of merchandise brought up the river from St. Louis, and tons upon tons of goods were often obliged to lie outside on the wharves, stacked up for several blocks, all awaiting transportation across the Plains by ox or mule power.

In the spring of 1860 the Pike's Peak gold excitement caused a tremendous rush, luring thousands of men from distant eastern sections. There was a perfect stampede to get to the "diggin's", it was a hungry crowd, and all their eatables had to come from the east by wagon train.

The south bank of the Platte river appears to have been commonly selected as the most feasible route over which these slow-moving caravans wended their way westward. It was no uncommon sight to see a string of freight wagons over a mile in length. For mutual protection while moving through the hostile Indian country these trains would generally travel together, as attacks could be expected at any time. The red man resented this intrusion into his territory, and mile after mile of it was watered with the blood of venturesome bull-whackers, mule-skinners and teamsters as the wary red man fought their stern advance.

Unquestionably the most famous of these freighting concerns was that of Russell, Majors & Waddell. The enormous wagons used by this firm were made to order, and during the height of their activities they employed no less than 6250 of these immense wagons, drawn by 75,000 oxen, counting in their relay stock. It is even stated that this firm used more oxen in their vast freighting business than all the other work oxen in the United States combined! Their wagons cost from $1000 to $1500 each, and where mules were employed, these animals cost from $500 to $700 a pair, while the harness for them amounted to from $300 to $600 a ten-mule team. Roughly speaking, a first-class freighting wagon outfit on the Plains in 1860 cost as much to furnish, ready for business, as does a Pullman car at the present time.

Alexander Majors — what a wealth of romance is connected with that name! — was the most noted man of finance operating in the Plains country in the freighting business. He was a strict Christian gentleman in every sense of the word. He would not hire a teamster, wagonmaster or mule-skinner without first requiring from the man a written agreement that he would neither swear, get drunk, gamble or mistreat his animals while in the employ of the company, no matter how great the provocation. None of the Russell, Majors & Waddell wagons ever moved out of camp on a Sunday. That day was one of rest for both men and animals, the men being paid just the same wage as if they were on the road. This added greatly to the popularity of this enterprising firm, and they never had any labor troubles to contend with.

For many years the Russell, Majors & Waddell firm had Government contracts for the transportation of military stores to all the various posts in the Far West. They were also extensively patronized by Brigham Young, the great Mormon leader, in transporting goods for him, as well as for many Salt Lake City merchants. The late Col. W. F.

Cody (Buffalo Bill) began his life on the Plains as a horse-herder for this great company.

The code of rules formulated by Alexander Majors for the behavior of his employes, read as follows:

"While I am in the employ of Russell, Majors & Waddell I agree not to use profane language, not to get drunk, not to gamble, not to treat animals cruelly, and not to do anything else that is incompatible with the conduct of a gentleman. And I agree that if I violate any of the above conditions to accept my discharge without any pay for my services."

Mr. Majors has stated that he never knew of a single instance of a man signing those "iron-clad rules" being discharged without his pay.

After the beginning of the Civil War, Mr. Majors still further requested every man in his employ to pay true allegiance to the Government of the United States, in addition to the foregoing rules and obligations.

It seemed to be the prevalent opinion at the time this firm began business that none but a class of "rough-necks" were fit to contend with the Indians and manage teamsters in these trips across the Plains; but Alexander Majors quickly proved that this was a mistaken fallacy.

With all the thousands of men in his employ, Mr. Majors has stated that he never had to do more than give a kindly rebuke in case of a misdemeanor to avoid a repetition of the offense.

"In all my business on the Plains," Mr. Majors relates, "I adhered as strictly as possible to keeping the Sabbath day and avoided traveling or doing any unnecessary work. When my men saw that I was just as willing to pay them the same wage as was paid by other firms who made their men work on Sunday, it gained me thousands of friends."

In 1858 the supplies which Russell, Majors & Waddell freighted to Utah were enormous, totaling more than 16,000,000 pounds, and requiring more than 3500 large wagons and 40,000 oxen and 4000 men to handle.

In the fall of 1860 Mr. Majors bought out his two partners and conducted the business alone under his own name.

During the summer and fall of 1864-5, the Indians were especially troublesome and their depredations constantly increasing. This was the time Chief Red Cloud, the great Sioux leader, was at the zenith of his career. Many of the smaller freighters were obliged to suspend business entirely, as it became a hard matter to find men who were willing to risk their scalps in the freighting business through the Indian country. This had a natural tendency to increase the cost of transporting merchandise across the Plains. The savages were in almost complete control of the highways; consequently the cost of groceries and necessities went skyrocketing. Transportation prices also soared skyward, until ordinary freight rates were advanced from nine to twenty-five cents a pound. In some instances certain commodities of a light and bulky nature cost as high as forty cents a pound to transport.

In July, 1864, there was such a plentiful supply of flour in the Denver markets that it sold at the mere cost of the freight—$9 a hundred. But so active had the Indians become by October of that year that flour soared to $40 a hundred, while a plain meal at a stage-station along the South Platte route, which heretofore had been obtainable at six bits, cost $2.

Finally the Government stepped in and ordered that all wagon trains must rendezvous at Fort Kearney, Nebraska, until at least twenty wagons and thirty men, thoroughly organized, were collected, before they would be allowed to pass Fort Kearney into the Indian country, with a captain over each company. By thus banding together the freighters were seldom molested in passing up and down the valley of the Platte river, being armed to the teeth and ready "for a feast, fight or frolic."

During the days of this overland trade it is estimated that there was on the Plains and in the mountains a floating population of nearly or quite 250,-000 persons. As but a comparatively few of the number made a pretense of raising anything in the shape of provender of any sort, most of it had to be transported from the distant east. The peak of this overland traffic was during the years between 1863 and 1866. The last year of the Civil War brought thousands into the western country, anxious to get away from a war devastated section and begin life anew. The gold camps of the West and Northwest caught the majority of these adventurers.

One of the greatest hardships encountered by the early-day freighters on the Plains was the absence of wood along a large portion of the route. For fully 400 miles along the Platte river fuel was indispensable and woefully scarce in some places. It frequently could be purchased at from $50 to $100 a cord. Between Cottonwood Springs and Denver, a distance of 300 miles, there was practically no fuel near at hand. Buffalo chips were commonly used — in fact, in the treeless sections it was the only fuel obtainable.

During 1865 it is stated that over 21,000,000 pounds of freight were shipped from Atchison alone. This vast total required 4917 wagons, 8164 mules, 27,685 oxen and 1256 men to handle.

The commerce of the prairies made great sums of money for those engaged in the traffic, and many of them besides Alexander Majors rolled up huge fortunes. With the advent of the iron horse, in 1869, freighting by wagons began to decrease, as did Missouri river traffic later, as branch railroads began reaching out into the unsettled sections of the West.

Today the "covered wagon" is but a remembrance of the old days on the Plains — days that were fraught with dangers and perils on every hand, but days which yet live in the memory of a few "old-timers" as the most romantic and wonderful days of their lives.

CHAPTER X

"REMEMBER THE ALAMO!"

MOST THRILLING DEFENSE IN AMERICAN HISTORY
TOOK PLACE AT SAN ANTONIO, TEXAS, MARCH 6, 1836

IN all the annals of American warfare, there are but two instances of battles fought from whence came no survivor.

These two instances were: the total annihilation of Gen. George A. Custer's battalion of five troops of cavalry, under his immediate command, June 25, 1876, in the battle of the Little Big Horn, in southeastern Montana; the other, the battle of the Alamo in what is today the city of San Antonio, Texas, on March 6th, 1836.

In this latter engagement, one hundred and eighty-three intrepid Texans, taking refuge in the Alamo, a mission church, surrounded by a high adobe wall, withstood for twelve successive days the assault of the combined forces of the Mexican army, numbering more than 6,000 troops, under command of Gen. Santa Anna. The daring defenders of the Alamo were eventually overpowered by the superior forces of the enemy, and slaughtered to a man, no quarter being asked or given. No more heroic defense was ever made in all the history of the warfare of the world than that of this devoted little band who sacrificed their lives within the old stone walls of the Alamo.

The struggle of Texas for independence forms one of the most thrilling chapters in American history. The Texans were in rebellion against Mexico during the early part of 1836. They desired a free provisional government, and were attempting, by force of arms, to establish their independence.

Early in February, 1836, Gen. Santa Anna was ordered north of the Rio Grande River to attempt to assert the authority of Mexico on that side of the river in what is now the state of Texas. Bexar (now known as San Antonio) was the objective point, and it was to be his mission to attempt to capture the town and put down the rebellion.

To hark back a bit: On the 10th of December, 1835, San Antonio was captured by the Texas patriots, who fought a spirited engagement against the Mexicans under General Cos, a brother-in-law of General Santa Anna. The Texans were under command of Gen. Burlinson. San Antonio was then garrisoned by about 1,700 Mexicans. The town itself contained a population of about 1,200. The Texans numbered only 216 men, but nevertheless, in spite of the overwhelming odds against them, they made a gallant attack, and for five days the siege was kept up, the Texans gaining ground at every encounter. The Mexicans were finally driven to the public square, or plaza. Here they had walled up the defenses and expected to make a most stubborn resistance. But the Texans were irresistible. They battered down the walls about the old plaza and drove the Mexicans into what had been a monastery, which was apparently secure against assault. But General Cos was short of provisions, and finally

ENTRANCE TO THE ROOM IN WHICH COL. JAMES BOWIE WAS SLAIN AT THE SIEGE OF THE ALAMO, MARCH 6, 1836. PAINTING OF DAVID CROCKETT OVER THE DOOR. PHOTO COURTESY H. L. SUMMERVILLE, SAN ANTONIO, TEXAS.

raised the white flag in token of surrender. It was a most fortunate move for the Texans, as their ammunition was completely exhausted. The Mexicans were given five days in which to retire, the officers to retain their side arms and private property; but all public property, ammunition and arms of the Mexicans was to be delivered to General Burlinson, leader of the Texans. The Mexicans had lost some 300 men, while the loss to the Texans had been but four killed and twenty wounded.

Among those who had joined the Texans in their fight for independence was the renowned Davy Crockett, from Tennessee, whose name will ever stand high on the scroll of immortal American frontiersmen. We shall have more to say later in the story about this intrepid rifleman, hunter and adventurer.

The defeat of General Cos was not received by Santa Anna with very good grace. He decided to move against San Antonio at once, and to assume command of the forces himself, vowing that he would wreak such a vengeance against the Texans that they would repent ever having attempted to assert their independence.

A word at this point regarding the Alamo: It was first established as the Alamo Mission by the Franciscan Friars in 1718. The word "Alamo" signifies "cottonwood," and it is stated that a grove of cottonwood trees originally surrounded the old mission. It is also said that the church originally possessed an arched roof, flanked on either side by square towers.

The Texans were thoroughly aroused and angered

by the invasion of their territory by Santa Anna and his 6,000 Mexicans. They were totally unprepared for the coming of the troops — indeed, the first tidings of their approach were heralded by sentinels posted on the roof of the old church. The Americans were under the command of Colonel William Travis, a native of North Carolina. He was a man of unquestioned courage and determination, a born leader and ready to die in defense of his country, where the supreme sacrifice demanded.

Upon the approach of Santa Anna's army, Travis ordered every man inside the Alamo, where he hoped to put up a strong defense until reinforcements could arrive. Associated with Travis was the renowned Colonel James Bowie, whose name is famous as the inventor of the bowie-knife, and David Crockett, the Tennessee backwoodsman, celebrated politician, unerring rifle shot, famous bear hunter, noted adventurer and romancer, who had come to Texas to cast his lot with Travis and his men in their fight for independence.

There was little time for the Texans to gather together much of anything in provisions or rations with which to sustain any prolonged siege. They had about a dozen pieces of artillery, but there was little ammunition for them. A few bushels of corn and some beef cattle were hastily gathered inside the high adobe wall surrounding the mission, and the Texans were ready to fight to the death.

Santa Anna made immediate demand for the surrender of the Alamo. A defiant refusal was the answer. The Mexicans at once raised a blood-red flag above their camp, signifying that no quarter was to be given the Americans.

Meanwhile, Travis had managed to start a messenger with appeals for assistance, to Colonel Fannin at Goliad; also to the provisional government at Washington, Texas. His stirring appeal is yet preserved in the archives at Austin, the capital of Texas. It read as follows:

"Fellow Citizens and Compatriots: I am besieged by a thousand or more Mexicans under Santa Anna. I have sustained a continued bombardment for 24 hours and have not lost a man. The enemy have demanded a surrender at discretion, otherwise the garrison is to be put to the sword if taken. I have answered with a cannon shot, and our flag still waves proudly from the walls. *I shall never surrender or retreat!* Then I call on you, in the name of liberty, of patriotism and of everything dear to the American character, to come to our aid with all dispatch. The enemy are receiving reinforcements daily, and will no doubt increase to 4,000 or 5,000 in three or four days. Though this call may be neglected, I am determined to sustain myself as long as possible and die like a soldier who never forgets what is due to his own honor and that of his country.

"Victory or death!"

"W. BARRETT TRAVIS,
"Lieut-Col. Commanding."

The messenger reached Colonel Fannin, and he did indeed set out from Goliad on the 28th of February, with 300 men and four pieces of artillery, but his outfit broke down when not more than a mile from the starting point. He had no provisions except a little rice and some dried beef, and seeing that he was not in form to render efficient service to Travis, he reluctantly returned to Goliad.

The provisional government was in session at Washington, Texas, on March 3d, 1836, when the last appeal of Travis for help was brought by messenger. Tremendous excitement followed its reading. One patriotic member suggested that the convention adjourn at once and march to the relief of the beleaguered garrison. In the midst of the excitement General Sam Houston arose. He said it was absolutely necessary that the convention continue its unfinished work of organizing a government, and that if the members would do this, he himself would climb into the saddle and start for the Alamo at once, gathering such forces as might be available on the way. His suggestion was greeted with outbursts of applause, and Houston left at once to organize a force of volunteers.

In order to let reinforcements know that he was still holding out, Colonel Travis had stated in his message that each morning he would fire a signal at sunrise. Houston was not able to reach the Alamo in time to assist, for the massacre had been completed.

During all this time the guns of Santa Anna's army were pounding away at the walls of the Alamo. On the 26th of February, Davy Crockett was awakened from a disturbed nap by bombs dropping near at hand. Snatching up his rifle, he made his way to a point where he could overlook the artillery fire. From this position he picked off, one after the other, six Mexicans as each approached the cannon to discharge it, silencing that gun completely.

Meanwhile, Travis was hoping against hope that his messenger had reached Washington, and that aid would be speedily forthcoming. But day after day passed with no sign of succor. On the 3d of March, Colonel Travis abandoned all hope that relief would arrive. During a lull in the firing, he assembled the garrison, telling them that he had something to say to them. The patriotic Texans gathered about him and he made a brief speech, stating that he had concluded aid would not reach them, and that unless it came within a very few hours their doom was sealed. He said it was his conviction that the messengers had been captured, else he felt sure their friends would have come to their defense several days previously. From now on it was to be every man for himself. As for him, he preferred to remain in the Alamo and fight to the death; the others were at liberty to do as they chose.

Then, drawing his sword, Colonel Travis marked a straight line across the adobe floor of the old mission. Stepping across it he said in firm, quiet tones:

"I wish every man who prefers to remain and die with me to cross this line."

Before the words had fairly left his mouth, every man who was able, stepped over the line. Davy Crockett fairly leaped over it in his enthusiasm. The Barrow brothers, twins, stepped over with their arms around each other's necks. The famous Colonel James Bowie was sick with typhoid fever, lying on a cot. As the men crossed the line drawn by

Travis, Bowie shouted: "Boys, I am not able to walk across that line, but will some of you be kind enough to lift me up and carry me over?" Willing hands complied with his request, while the sick and incapacitated men, with patriotic fervor, feebly arose and tottered after him, while those unable to walk were carried across by enthusiastic comrades.

Where is there a parallel of such heroism in all the annals of American history? Not a man faltering! Every patriotic Texan resolved to die rather than surrender or retreat! The names of those one hundred and eighty-three men should be written in letters of gold on a monument of enduring construction.

It has been stated that every man responded to Colonel Travis' appeal. There was one single exception. A man named Moses Rose preferred to take his chances of escaping from the garrison, and as the others crossed the line, he alone, with head downcast and his face hidden in his hands, remained behind, a picture of helplessness and despair. Observing his agitation, Bowie exclaimed:

"You seem unwilling to die with us, Rose."

"But I am not prepared to die," exclaimed the despairing man, "and I shall not if I can make my escape."

Davy Crockett was bending over the cot of Bowie in earnest conversation. As Rose uttered these words, Crockett said, in cheerful but determined tones:

"You can't escape, old man. You might as well make up your mind to that and remain and die with the rest of us."

But Rose shook his head. Hastily gathering a few possessions together, he actually managed to scale the wall undetected and escape down the river.

The siege continued until the 6th of March. On that day Santa Anna had arrived at the conclusion that he had lost both time and men enough by former methods of fighting, and he resolved to take the Alamo by assault. Twenty-five hundred men constituted the storming party. They were drawn up in four columns and supplied with scaling ladders, axes and other implements to cross the walls and batter in the doors of the Alamo. In the rear of the infantry the cavalry was formed, not to aid in the assault, but to hem in and drive forward the infantry in case they hesitated or were driven back. The artillery was in command of Gen. Castrillion. Santa Anna and his staff secured advantageous positions where they could watch the unequal contest. The regimental band accompanied them.

It was just daybreak when the bugles sounded the advance, the band playing "El Duguelo," signifying "no quarter." The scaling party placed their ladders against the walls and prepared to advance. And now the Texans, with ringing shouts of defiance, turned their unerring rifles against the invaders, and so deadly was their fire that time and again the scaling party was driven back, only to be urged forward by saber blows in the hands of the cavalry and their own officers.

What a dramatic scene was that! Intermingled with the roar of artillery, the crack of the long-barreled muzzle-loading rifles in the hands of the Texans and the rattle of the Mexican musketry, came the shouts of the combatants, while high over all echoed the wailing notes of the bugle calls and the blare of the band.

But human endurance has a limit. The garrison was worn out with exhaustion, wounds, sickness and hunger. How could Travis and his patriotic little band hope to withstand the assaults of thirty times their own numbers? All knew they must die at some point in the struggle. It had been agreed when the situation became critical and all hope was gone, that the powder magazine should be exploded and all perish together. But Colonel Evans, while attempting to perform this duty, was shot down at the door of the magazine, torch in hand.

One by one the gallant little band succumbed. Colonel Travis had been killed during the first hour of the storming of the garrison, meeting his death like the true hero he was, while standing on the wall cheering on his men. But before he fell he had met, in personal encounter, General Munro, in charge of the storming party, and in a desperate hand-to-hand encounter, each had expired at the hands of the other.

Davy Crockett, the invincible rifleman, met his death with a smile upon his face. He was found dead in an angle, lying on his back, his battered and broken rifle at his side and his knife in his hand, with a dead Mexican across his body and twenty-two more lying piled in the angle. Crockett had certainly extracted a fearful toll from Santa Anna's forces!

Colonel James Bowie was, as has been stated, lying sick with typhoid fever on a cot, unable to rise and fight. He was a famous pistol shot, and from his sick cot he brought down many of his foes before his ammunition was expended, after which he fought with the knife he had already made famous. It is stated that he slew nearly a dozen Mexicans before a bullet crashed through his head.

At length only a mere half dozen of the defenders remained alive, and General Castrillion was in favor of sparing their lives; but his appeal to Santa Anna was met with a stern refusal and the reply that no quarter should be given any individual. A defiant shout from the Texans was answered with a volley from the foe, and the massacre was complete.

There remained alive to tell the story of this heroic struggle, five human beings, none of whom took any part in the defense of the Alamo. These were the wife and child of Lieut. Dickinson, who himself died with his comrades, a negro servant of Col. Travis and two Mexican women. The lives of these five were spared.

The bodies of the brave defenders were gathered into a great heap during the day, and after being stripped and all valuables appropriated, they were burned in one huge fire.

The story of a Mexican fifer named Polin Saldigua, a boy of 16, forms an interesting feature of the defense of the Alamo. It is stated that among others he was allowed to enter the blood-spattered mission after the Texans had all been killed. Santa Anna had ordered that none of the bodies of the combatants should be disturbed until he had personally looked upon the scene and noted just how each had fallen. He had employed three or four of the leading citizens of San Antonio to enter the fighting area with him and point out the bodies of several of the leading Texans who had fallen in the slaughter. Santa Anna specified that he was especially desirous of viewing the bodies of Colonel Travis, Colonel Bowie and one other man, whose description, says Saldigua, left no doubt but that he referred to Davy Crockett.

Saldigua stated that upon entering the fort, a scene lay spread before them which more resembled a slaughter house than anything else. The bodies of the Texans lay as they had fallen, and heaps of dead Mexicans were piled indiscriminately about and upon them. It had been a hand-to-hand engagement at the end, and bodies were thickly strewn about. Santa Anna and his staff wandered about the interior for some time, stepping over and upon the bodies as it suited their fancy, and apparently enjoying their sickening butchery with delight.

Finally the body of Colonel Travis was discovered. After Santa Anna had viewed the face and form of the dead leader, he drew his sword, thrust it through the body and turned away. That of Crockett was next viewed and similarly disfigured.

Finally several other officers came into the bloody arena, and after a conference with Santa Anna the latter retired. A squad was then detailed to lay the bodies of all the Texans in one large pile. Two of the officers then took stand in the middle of the main area. The first corpses were brought and laid as the officers directed. This formed a nucleus for the pile. The bodies were each brought in by four men and dropped near the feet of a Mexican captain.

In imitation of Santa Anna this officer viewed each body and then thrust his sword through it, after which it was cast upon the pile.

When all the bodies had been collected, several soldiers, with cans of camphene, walked around them, pouring the fluid upon them and thoroughly saturating them. A match was then cast upon the pile and the flame instantly shot to a great height. The detail continued its work until the bodies had been consumed.

The news of the slaughter at the Alamo aroused all Texas to a furious fighting pitch, and every man was eager to battle for the independence of his beloved territory. Within three weeks after the great tragedy a thousand frontiersmen flocked to join the army which General Sam Houston was raising, his headquarters being near the site of the present city of Austin.

On the 21st of April, and with a force of 650 men, Gen. Houston met Santa Anna with a force of 1,600 Mexicans on the banks of the San Jacinto River. The battle lasted but an hour or so, and was one of the most desperate hand-to-hand encounters on record. The battle cry of the Texans was *"Remember the Alamo!"* under the inspiration of which the Texans fought with a fury unequaled. The American forces lost 241 men killed, while the Mexican loss was 580 killed and wounded. Eight hundred prisoners were taken, Santa Anna himself being among them. It required strenuous efforts on the part of General Houston to prevent the frenzied Texans from dealing with the Mexican leader as he had

dealt with Travis, Crockett, Bowie and the other
defenders of the Alamo.

Today the Alamo is shown to tourists and visitors with genuine patriotic pride. No more desperate resistance was ever made in the face of overwhelming numbers than that which took place
within the walls of this historic old building, bap-
tized with the blood of the most heroic band of
Americans that ever pulled a trigger in the es-
tablishment of a provisional free government.

THE "ALAMO," SAN ANTONIO, TEXAS.